T0167667

RESISTANCE IS FUTILE

Also by John Gallas from Carcanet

Flying Carpets over Filbert Street
Grrrrr

JOHN GALLAS

Resistance is Futile

CARCANET

First published in 1999 by
Carcanet Press Limited
4th Floor, Conavon Court
12-16 Blackfriars Street
Manchester M3 5BQ

A CIP catalogue record for this book
is available from the British Library
ISBN 1 85754 404 8

The publisher acknowledges financial assistance
from the Arts Council of England

Set in 10pt Horley Old Style by Bryan Williamson, Frome
Printed and bound in England by SRP Ltd, Exeter

Contents

Yoghurt

It was a frisky day in Ulan Bator.
Hoo Gerjan hurried down October Street.
The wind worried the skirts of his duck-coat.
It was Spring: he frowned.
It was not that he disliked Spring.
He screwed up his face, which was inclined to fat.
He turned into Paradise Bypass.
It was just that he was in a bit of trouble.

He climbed the stairs.
His big fingers squeezed the handrail.
The door said: 'Guriltai. LLF. DDDDD. X.
Reasonable Solicitor'.
He rang the bell: it buzzed.

'It is not in dispute,' said Mr Guriltai,
'that you stole this car.'
Hoo Gerjan scowled. The sun shone
through the third floor window
and a kettle steamed.
Mr Guriltai cleaned his ear while he waited.
'No,' said Hoo.
'Several hundred people, if I am not wrong,'
said Mr Guriltai, looking at his finger,
'saw you do it.'
Hoo nodded in an ugly way.
A sheet of black hair dropped over his eyes
and he pushed it away.
'Tea?' said Mr Guriltai.

'Do you like your apartment?'
Hoo smiled widely.
'Not especially particularly,' he said.
'Then I have a plan,' said Mr Guriltai.

When they asked him his name
Hoo Gerjan replied, 'Yoghurt.'
Also his address and date of birth.
They demanded his version of events
and Hoo replied, 'Yoghurt.'
The magistrates shouted.
Mr Guriltai raised his eyes to the ceiling.
'This is your last chance,' said the magistrates.
The sun shone the shape of a window
on their desk.
'Yoghurt,' said Hoo.

He was locked in a small bedroom for six months.
The heating stayed on until May
and he put on a little weight.
But mostly he sat on his bed
wrapped up in his duck-coat
and looked out the window
at the sky.

When he was released
Hoo went back to Paradise Bypass.
He climbed the stairs.
He had to stop half way up to catch his breath.
The door still said: 'Guriltai. LLF. DDDDD. X.
Reasonable Solicitor.'
He rang the bell: it buzzed.

'Come in, come in!' said Mr Guriltai, smiling.
'Would you like tea?'
Hoo looked at him in a fat sort of way.
It was snowing outside.
The window panes were iced up
except for a melted hole in the middle.
Mr Guriltai blew his nose and fiddled with his spoon.
'That wasn't too bad now was it?' he said.
A kettle steamed.
'And what do you say to this very reasonable fee?'
He pushed a piece of paper across the table.

Hoo looked at it rudely.
'Yoghurt,' he replied.

His apartment was dark and cold.
Snow had fallen in an icy pile
beside the rubbish bin.
He looked down at the car park.
There were six policemen there.

*

3   1s

1

Tears are a flood where fleas live.

2

More than dust, less than rust.

3

Trust in God but lock your bike.

*

Museum with Samuel Beckett's Telephone

Voici by God the telephone
brisk black bakelite which is
the last word happily commensurate
with durable employment

bolt through brittle yellow paper

Dial 12 for Information Complaints
is charmingly 13 14 what Telegraph
Police immediate rescue 17 good dash
Fire Brigade dingding and water 18

tail cut off no answer still

*

Bush

The sun was going. Horses squish-squash-squished
along the rotty track; the river way
below awhisper. Beech like hairs on Hopeless'
scalp. Zig, a zag, a zig. Rain-piss,
ooze; blackish, dripping fernflags. Day
gave up. Down, down they went. 'I wished

we was there.' Branches spat a load
across his shoulders. 'Shit.' They were six:
small-tall-tall-tall-dead-thin, a carry-hack
and two blue dogs. Horses tiptoed. Black
pinch-pools and puddles haared with silt and flicks
of gold. The fast-glass river. In they rode.

The thin one gobbed; 'Shut yer grizzlin Cack.'
They stamped the drowned-round stones and zig-zagged up.
Somewhere Heaven, sooty-cold. Bush
wrapped the earth, twice-rained the rain. 'Shush!'
They stopped. Horsebreath; leafslap. 'Nope.' 'Hup-hup.'
'Aint nuffing.' Cough. Push on. The endless track.

They peeked the gloom behind. The body's boots
bumped, and little Cack saw hats in stones.
'Aint nuffing left.' Its bubbling dungarees
hung up a small black hole. Up up; the trees
found high-clear. 'Stop.' The thin one gobbed. 'Oi, Beaunes –
there's light.' They gulped the giant sky. Beechroots

grabbed at blots of space. A tree-sea nightmare
heaved at nothing, on and on. Cold rain
aired down. 'Less go.' One by one they left
the ridge and drowned in leaves. The darkling weft
like magic passed them through a speargrass plain
beyond the light. They turned around. 'We's there.'

Fat sheep slept in smelly clouds between
their now and soon. Beaunes went first, their hats
like funnels. 'Look.' The candle-beacon bowed:
a papered wall stepped out in roses. Ploughed
mud and bracken, droppings. Cross dim flats
of docked-down grass. 'Bestest sight I seen,'

hissed Beaunes. The tall man smiled. Rotted straw
bestrewed the earth. 'They got hot water? Shit,
I need a tub.' The thin man gobbed; 'Damn,
they aint got –' 'Shush!' The horses steamed. A lamb
floated on the steps and stared. 'Hey, Squit,
do nice and interduce us to the door.'

A Muir & Pippit panted on a thread
behind his sackshirt, blankets, oilskin, grin.
Neighbour-knocks. A bird-scream. Nothing. Rain.
Knock knock knock. Screech-squawk. The window pane
whummed. *Knock-knock knock-knock.* The light went in
and flimmered doorwards. 'This ere man is dead,'

said Beaunes. 'I wonders if youd let im lay –'
he touched his heart – 'is relics somewhere clean.'
He waved his teeth. 'Come in.' They dripped inside.
Wooden boxes piled high, drilled and tied
with flaxrope pinking, beaks and claws. 'You been
travlin far?' 'We come from Orseleg Bay.'

Cack and Carey gawped at Beaunes. 'We got –'
He hissed at them in secret. 'Put im there.
Thems my birds. I sell em.' Carey gobbed.
'It aint no night for travlin.' 'We was robbed,'
said Cack. 'Shit, we ad a –' – secret – 'Where?'
'Up Orseleg Creek.' Dogs yammered. 'Ee were shot.'

'This eere man' said Beaunes, 'were Robbie Drew.
Me an im come west wiv Squit and Piggin
jobbin. Carey narks us bout this place,'
he squinty-winked, 'forgot its name.' His face
bloomed with teeth. 'Cack come too: for diggin.'
'Gold,' said Cack. A box-bird hollered. True.

'We spected months up Orseleg Creek' (lie,
said Cack to Cack) 'an tented round the Bay
an plumbed a strike.' A kea heeked. 'We done
free months. Ee kept the slabbies wiv is gun.
We trusts im. Shit, they shot im on the skidway
an dumped im down the mullock-bank to die.'

'Me an Piggin found im,' (true) squirmed Squit.
'They robbed us gold,' said Cack. The bird-man chewed
his baccy: 'Well, youse welcome for the night.'
They slept on bracken beds. Weak candlelight
blinked on steamy cheeks. Dark boxes cooed.
The black bush dripped: crackle-dreams, steam-lit.

Wet and reeky, morning billed by shags.
They dug up porridge. Squit went out to piss.
He broke the Muir & Pippit, ran two shots
and dropped it in his shirt. Rain twittered knots
of fern and scrub and doled an endless hiss
across the greyworld. Piggin humped the bags

and winked. The tall men left to find the law.
A whispering tote-tin rode in Beaunes' poke.
Through danky windows Cack and Carey eyed
their expedition wasting. Fantails cried;
wet clouds unmoved. Carey gobbed. Greensmoke
dribbed. The body darkened on the floor.

Propped on shuffling, whispering crates, they slept.
The bird-man took his nag to traps. The sky
went black and blue and green. Darkness dropped
in thrown tarpaulins. Now! The tall men stopped
and turned their horses. Tuis tried to fly
before them, noosed and sopping. Blue dogs crept

like eels through punga boles. 'Oi, Carey.' 'What?'
'I eard somefing.' Carey gobbed. Scud
and rack made luminous by something beaked.
'I godda shit.' The flowing beechsea streaked
with mizzle, watching. Cack splosh-crossed the mud.
They waited, pokers in the blackbush rot.

The moon was smothered. 'Gennilmen, less go.'
They jingled blindly past the speargrass plain.
Cack crackled down. He heard the duckboards swoosh
and rain fell on his nerves. He shucked the bush
like mushy boots and flew. The window pane
filled up with faces; roses; emberglow;

sleep-snuffling. Beaunes slipped through the door. Sou'wester
dribbled; bougie in each hand; his hat
steamed. The roses' ruddy glowgleam smoked.
He crumpled out. *Woodpile!* – Piggin poked
his finger – *down there!* Drizzle, pitapat.
Squit struck up the bougies with a vesta.

He oozed inside the floor-drop. Piggin slopped
white-whisky on a mitt; Squit dragged it in.
Beaunes saw the blabless bush spit endlessly
at earth. Squit squirrelled out. 'I done it.' Three
tall men all waited tally. Fluttering spin
of yellow light – it licked – the woodpile popped.

Blowing sweet, freshfire cupped the shack
like something's hand and burned with boiling rotsteam
up the walls. Sheets of roof-tin fizzed
and skewed up wings. Clout-head broadsides whizzed
from use to thing. 'Less go.' Gusty flamegleam
made them giants. They turned. The bush stretched black.

Cack woke up: dead and gone to Hell!
Flames flew up outside the glass; squeeze-sap
squirted at his boots. The bracken bierbeds
seethed and paper roses blistered reds.
The boxes screeched; booming, sudden fearflap.
Cack's hair disappeared. Feathers fell.

The walls collapsed. Little Cack fell through,
his clothes on fire and like a foundry press
the roof stamped down and minted things from souls.
Cack peeled in a mudbank. Stars made holes
in nothing. Smoke up-drizzled with a mess
of ashes in its arms, and rain hacked through.

Piggin, Squit and Beaunes reached Bellbird Bogs
three days after. Milk-electric bunchlight,
scadsy smell. 'Bestest sight I seen,'
hissed Beaunes. Squishsquash down the gully. Greasegreen
flumes, berdans, batteries, drays. Night
spewed them wound up Bank Street, and the dogs.

They slept in soapy sheetbliss. Fug-warm damped
through Greens Hotel. 'You recknin up now boys?'
Squit sneered; 'Wes goin to the bank – an get
some monkeys.' Piggin hoicked. The world all wet,
mashed mud and soot. CASHHERE TOPRATES. Thumpnoise
in the gully; diggers; thump. They stamped

16

down duckboards to the door. Three hats scoured through.
Beaunes unsheathed his teeth. 'This ere's gold.'
He drew the tote-tin. 'Pay me.' Shaveslick pink,
clean-clobbered, grogstewed, Strike Saloon, clink clink:
'Threehunnidanninepouneightansix!' A cold
double: glass to Carey, Cack and Drew!

The bird-man bobbed still-stiff. Beaunes sparked cigars.
Icy water rattled traps all tangled
round his braces. Squit fell off: he squealed
laugh-laugh. The nag squished down the dockgrass field:
spitsplit smoke, broke-out sheep, mangled
charwood, ruin. Drizzle put out stars.

Three days they grogged and always thud-thud-thud,
earstamp, bloodcrush, souldig. 'Jee-zus!' Squit
squirmed and jiggled teeth like crushing stones.
Morning bled the hotel blinds white. Beaunes
sipped his egg, 'We's leavin,' snapped a biscuit.
'Get two jackers.' Indian file through mud.

Beaunes new yellow monkey-jacket: Skull,
the dog: Squit and Piggin tweeded: Cutlass,
dog: Doll, for digging: Easy Blodstett,
grubstake: carry-hack: mud: hoofholes: bushwet:
empty track. The gully-water hiss
faded. Bellbirds clear, earth echo-dull.

Thumping soon became their hearts. Bushseas
ebbed and flowed for weeks. The sky ripped:
a cold blue ceiling. Doll shy-shivered. Rotted
roots, ice-stones, splashing toi-toi, blotted
ferns, ever and ever, cold blue dripped,
westwards, on and on. Dreadful trees

gigantic passed slow-ship-like in a gloom
shot with vicious blue. They climbed. The topwood
gaped and found sea splashing thunder-grey
the blackdrawn beach. Beaunes sparked up: 'Codders Bay.'
The ocean spread grey-leagued to Hope: they stood,
shivering smiles, and heard its high-hushed boom.

Easy Blodstett pulled his spyglass. Spindrift
shifts glittered over ironsand. 'Gerd.'
He tugged his cap. Codders Bay out-bowed
between mud mullheads whipped with scrub. They rode
slow down. Nikau boles bulged, and blurred
blue clarity beyond. Shags cawed. Doll sniffed.

Hooves hit sand, black foamy. Prickling cold
danced the surf. Skull snapped water. Squit
stared: all-grey, ever-drawn curtain. Swoosh,
swoosh. Cutlass wagged his tail. Bush
ganged behind, dead-dripping. 'Holy shit,'
said Doll. Sea ate their boots. 'This aint gold.'

Beaunes squeezed up his eyes and frowned. Somewhere
past the sea was damned content. He whistled:
blue dogs slithered on the southern head.
Herons wound the wind. Piggin led
the hack-horse in a hollow. Broadleaf bristled
clack like sticks. Squit fished out a pair

of spotted snotrags. 'Put em on.' Along
the drench-grass neck, a traverse bushline track,
jet green and brilliant blue. Blindfold Doll
and Easy Blodstett trailed the right-ear roll
of surf and cold-face sky. It faded. Clack
of stone-scree: wind: a thin creek's ripple-song.

The horses upped. Wind new-nipped their faces.
Pebbles pushed like monstrous sand. Night
was darker darkness. Doll sleeprode. Push on.
Steeper. Up. Stacking shingle shone.
They stopped. The early skyroof quick raw white.
'Take em off.' Mullock heaps; cut races;

dams and sluices; splashdown creeks. 'Whirr,'
Easy Blodstett smiled, 'are why?' Beaunes
dismounted. 'Nowheres what you'd know.' Drops
teetered out on rotten beechbranch props
tipping barksheets; riffles cracked with stones;
slewing sheepskin mould; mudded slur

spludged obstruction down the gullied hills.
They loaded off and runned the tents and blacked
billy. Piggin, Squit and Beaunes tramped
the creeks, booted flowdead races, stamped
the drypools. Little Cack's tincup whacked
fireblack off a treenail. Silted spills

fanned freezing water. Dams dribbled. Squit
shouldered shovels. 'Get them buggers clear.'
They dug. Doll whistled. Then he didn't. Sun
lulled up the sky. Waterbulges spun
freeforward, dam to dam. The draggled smear
of rainmouths steamed. The races raced. 'Shee-it!'

Doll bucked his teeth and whooped. They banked the flow,
logged dams. Summer sniffled warm. Pipes pushed
the current sluicewards. Blue dogs snoozed on hot
white boulders. Trees new green. The creekfall shot
three drops, splish-splashed the riffles, hissed and swooshed
like wings away. 'Gennilmen, less go.'

Three shut years they scratched the hill and bust
their hearts for gold. Each hundred-counted day
Squit rode out with Easy Blodstett's cash
to Croesus Pass for grub. The brainblank bash
of shovels, bushspooks, deadmouth, gutspike, gloomgrey,
airfright, souldrop, fever, rot and rust

clogged them, ghosts and shadows. Easy Blodstett
slept with glittered bottles, pillow-flour
and beantins scared and dreamed of Bellbird Bogs:
Beaunes and Squit lay empty-straight, blue dogs
twitching: Doll and Piggin, thin and sour,
crooked like bits of string, distilled in sweat.

High snows melted. Squit turned back from ooze
and floods. The grub ran out. They boiled bark
and billied birds' eggs. Water sloshed the races,
shooting gravel. Five worn fire-flush faces
lamped inside the night marooned by dark
fast lines of water drilled with godblack rimus.

Easy Blodstett said they had enough:
sixteen bottles. Beaunes eyed Squit through sparkspit.
Doll said let's go home. Piggin licked
his lips. Flame-eyes wound and peered. Beaunes kicked
burnt branches, blazebits' crack and whirl. 'Shit,
we ain't rich –' 'We ain't –' 'Shush!' Windpuff.

Creak. The dogs bristled. Dark uphill
like birdy whirr. Creak. Two treetops mudweak
reeled and little Cack's tincup jangling
keeled colossal whistling down: dangling
roots whipped up and all with air-rip shreik
trenched the scree and fire and juddered still.

Doll breathed bubbles. Boxed in floodthrown stones
he rolled off slowly cold along the bank;
head-down through the bed he passed and saw
white floating rocks and golden slabbies pour
with treacly ease around him while he drank
long spears of water launched from clouds. 'Beaunes!'

'Iss bard.' Easy Blodstett picked his beard.
Ashrags swirled. 'Beaunes! For chrissakes! Fuck!'
Piggin seesawed; trunk-skelfs nailed his knee
against a sluice-stand. Beaunes lamped the tree.
He turned to Squit. 'Where's Spadebrain?' 'Shit! I'm stuck!
Jeez!' Squit rubbed his face; one side was smeared

with scalds of billyboil and mud. One eye
puffshut and pink. Dogs yapped at the smash.
Squit squinted; 'Saves a pea.' Shush! They humped
the snarl off Piggin. Bloody britches; slumped
inside his tent. Wraithed with crudded ash
the others watched from rocks the freshets. Sky

bruising purple. Nothing. Soon the light.
'Drarned,' said Squit. Beaunes smiled. 'Mirr firr ars,'
Easy Blodstett spat and splashed away.
Across its watery compass hauled the day.
Nothing. Easy Blodstett packed his jars.
'We's goin ome,' said Beaunes. He winked. 'Ginnight.'

'You reckon ees asleep?' Drip-dripping tent.
Squit was shaking. 'Don't much matter.' Drip.
Drip. 'I only got two peas.' He hugged
the Muir & Pippit. 'Two's enough.' Beaunes shrugged.
'I can't see good.' Beaunes bared his teeth. Plip-plip,
plip-plip. 'I'm goin.' Squit hiked the flaps and went –

'Jeez!' Dripping, dumb and bogey-white
Doll pitched in and flopped flapbang. 'Now!
Do it! Now!' spat Beaunes. Squit ripped outside.
Gulp; the world, the floodblack roar. Cockeyed
he rattled, shingle socks aslither. Ow.
The Muir & Pippit, do it, do it – right:

he ripped the tentflaps. Easy Blodstett's eyes
bored like nailheads. Jammed against the backsheet,
sixteen bottles strung across his heart
and wide awake. 'Dern shirt: you brerk dim.' Smart.
The bottles crazed Squit's aim. With every beat
of fright the gold like flicks of fizzing sandflies

burbled up in twinkling squirts. *Blam*!
The woodcrutch burst. Bottles jingle-jangled.
Squit barged dazzled down the tent and stuck
the gun in Easy Blodstett's ear. Fuck.
Balloony billows, canvas stampballs tangled
softly Squit and *Bang*! and *splatter*. Damn.

The tent flopped up and died. Wombwound, black,
Squit baffed the kissing canvas sticky-dripped
and bloody backed outside. 'Gimmee booooots!'
Eggstones warped and clattered, rimu roots
ricked his toes. Shit. The bottles slipped
and squealed. 'Beaunes! For chrissakes! Take em!' Crack.

One gone. Beaunes was waiting. 'Gimmee those.
Take yer orse.' Doll sat up; his tongue
wax-swollen. Water dribbled down his vest.
'Yer boots.' His eyes flapped shut: his kitten chest
bobbed. He gagged. 'Gogo!' The brownie slung
its hooves for southwards through the dawn-made shadows.

'We jus bin robbed.' 'I eard em.' Doll sneezed snot.
'Squit's after em.' 'I eard.' 'An Easy's croaked.'
'I fort so.' Beaunes rat-scouted Doll's oozed eyes.
'We's goin.' Doll's eyes smiled. Beaunes spat. Sunrise
lit the tents like paper lamps. Doll choked
and hiccupped. Beaunes retreated. 'Ee were shot.'

'I fort so.' Beaunes was gone. Trees steamed. He rolled
the bottles up his squab. Cutlass snapped
at string. The floodcreeks leapfrogged. Piggin stood
and watched. 'We goin now?' Beaunes nodded. 'Good.'
Sunshine cleared the bush. Doll smiled. They wrapped
Easy Blodstett in his tent. Gold

flickered on his fingertips; his cashkey
palled in canvas. Doll sat trussed in blankets
by the sluicewreck with a sun-spun halo
round his head. 'Gennilmen, less go.'
They mounted up and clattered out through bits
of riffles, props and dams towards the sea.

Squit turned back at Fleabite Falls; the track
floundered full of slime. He stowed the gun
and slogged on east above the spew to Blaze
and turned north-west. Two weeks. New long days
warmed the bush. They crossed the Cloudies: sun
slithered saddle-snow: traversed crick-crack

the icy pitch and down. The others trotted
Codders Bay and watched the waves run in.
Horses splashed up greywash; turned away
along the northern mudmull webbed in spray.
Bush gulped them. Beaunes: the body bumped: Piggin:
hump-back: droopy Doll: blue dogs. Knotted

palmroots skysnatched; fluttering sunleaves; on
and on. Trunktides backwards winding. Weeks.
The dry track boomed. Limebright roof-green trailed
the slow blue sky; giant totaras sailed
between. Doll wobbled, water-weak. Creeks
burbled warm retreat. The scrub-sea shone.

Beaunes' ruined yellow monkey-jacket topped
the trees. More trees. They crossed the speargrass plain
and three warm days. Sunset fired up tired-tin
rooves and glitter glaze. They clattered in.
Beaunes cranked about to Doll; 'Ome again.'
His teeth glared. Doll spooled his eyes. They stopped.

The gold machines stood still: Bellbird Bogs'
gone-thumper heart. Brokedown shacks. Bank Street.
Clunked corrugated-iron. The fan-sun bled
away. Heaven at last. Wood blew red.
They rode to Greens with shadows. Monstrous dustsheet
hung its front with ghosts. 'Old them dogs.'

Beaunes got off. 'I's goin in.' He threw
the sheetedge. Cutlass yowled. The grubstake's hack
skittered: shroudfeet bumped at Beaunes' roll.
Piggin gobbed. Nothing. No one. Doll
swayed in duskwarm blank. The bush blurred black.
They waited. Gloombirds piped: drew-drew, drew-drew.

Hope: no more. Drew-drew, drew-drew. Green
verandah peel. GR_EN_ board. Beaunes flung forth
and flared his teeth. 'Shee-it. There ain't no law.
There ain't no nuffing.' Smiles. 'One Chinkee-chaw,
some fuckface down the dark. They's all struck north.'
He spied the nothing. 'Bestest sight I seen.'

They dug a hole behind the church and dumped
the body, helled by lightfire. Beadys Pass.
Squit's wee brownie wag-and-jingle waited
up the hill. Sparks ticked. Deathshovels grated
holy gravelearth. God-coloured glass
hemmed the moon. 'Less go.' Rag-Doll slumped

against the piss-wall. 'Goldrush! Jeez!' Beaunes grinned.
They trotted out. The bush like sleep reached down
to take them, horses, men and dogs. The moon
sailed out. Their billycocks – now Squit's too – soon
faint-flittered through the cream flood, greeny-brown
and sank. Bracken whispered in the wind.

Bourne put down his spyglass. Dark draped through
Greens upstairs red saloon. How snap the stars.
He stood up, tightpain-hobbled. 'Hickee!' Shit.
They sat and smoked; Bourne raised his veil. The moonlit
white verandah gulped the sheet. Kakas
hacked and tooted. Snoutreek silver-blue.

'They gorn up Beadys Pass you reckon?' 'Ha.'
'Jus like all them others.' 'Ha.' 'You tellem?'
'Ha.' Nod nod nod. 'Good guns.' He peeled
his gloves. The moon dropped light; chairs creaked. 'They stealed
my shovel.' Hickee squeered. 'I saw em.' Moondim
dust ballooned up Bank Street. 'Get the Soldier.'

Hickee scampered through the street. 'Whoozair?'
Oozair oozair bounced back Bank Street. Something
scuttled. Hickee cocked the Soldier. Duckboards
clacked: closer, closer, gawk-towards
the white verandah, blankets strapped with string,
drooped Doll. 'They've took is boots.' Blockblank despair

limped his eyes at Hickee's gun. 'Wait!
Wait.' They sat him down the Strike Saloon:
sunshine, sheepbroth, fatsoap, ropeshirt, shush.
Lightsquares crisscrossed floorboards; fat-green bush
blew up outside and pleached. Each afternoon
they walked him arms-and-shoulders up the creekspate

brimmed by piupius, broom and cress that quicked
his heart with some blunt dread. A month. The sky
blared in brilliant blankness. Bourne and Hickee
rugged him up against a cabbage-tree
and worked the rustcramp stamper. Goldswag kowhai
itched up midair tuis; waxeyes pricked

in honeybells. Thump. Thump. The stampfeet.
Doll stood up. The creekleap glittered. Noise
seen, light heard: he thumbed the Soldier. 'Look!'
Bourne stopped his handle. Rockspoil cracked. Doll took
the gun and waded in. He stared. Turquoise
waterglass and moss-stones drove his heartbeat:

Bang. He chucked it in. The water slurped
his knees. Bedstones slowly clunked. 'Shit,'
he watched his lensing fishfeet, 'this ain't gold.'
Autumn withered. Doll got yakky. Cold
raindays roofed the bush. Hugged in a blanket,
bloodberry stained, he poked the stove and chirped

while rainswing rat-tat-tatted Greens' tin tops.
Bourne walked the kitchen hat and veil all ears.
Hickee salted pig. 'You say this place?
Huh?' Doll looked up. Blackcurtain face.
'You been here?' Doll looked round. Homesick tears
flicked his eyes. Across the windows wind-drops

flew and splattered. 'Why'd they leave you? Eh?'
Shit. 'Where you bin?' Winter locked
the bush. Twenty rot-froze rooms. They slept
like hedgehogs and the blindwhite deadworld swept
from sea to sea like sea. Gasp-doors knocked
and squealed. Someone came and rode away

but no one saw; and with him went the sway
of winter. Shimmer-drizzle shot with lime;
dripping water; Doll wrapped in his rug.
Hickee chopped; slugferns unrolled; Bourne dug
the splodgebank lagged with flourbags. Strakes of greenslime
gooed the stones. He slipped. Doll watched the grey

glass nightmare mount his white-dam back and suck.
The firewood fell, smacking at the bushskirt
with its arms. He jumped. He waded in.
He grabbed Bourne's belt; he grabbed his hands; the skin
lumped and lop like coldwax; grabbed his shirt
and lugged him out. 'Doan look.' Doll dropped him. 'Fuck.'

Moonlight blanched the white verandah. Smokescat
looped the Strike Saloon. The long-bust barglass
mirrored six. 'Them questions what you arst.'
Bourne looked up. 'You arnsrin?' 'Might be.' Wormcast
head. 'Them two what rid up Beadys Pass:
where'd they come from?' Doll struck up and spat.

'I knows I'm ome. Bangs an me drunked ere
a farsend times. I knows that fump-fump-fump;
I got this winder-view by eart; I seen
them trees; I eard them birds ding-dong; I been
upstairs; I been down Peek's; I been to Blackstump.
Bangsey fruzz to deaf up Cloudy Clear.

An then these crashers come, them ones you seen
what brung me ome. They ad a pile of gold' –
Bourne leaned forward – 'No one never saw it.'
'What's their names?' 'Piggin, Beaunes an Squit.'
Bourne sat back and spat. 'They never told
no one where they digged. I never been

in no one's experdition. When they brassed
them flicks they come in ere an shouts the lot
an drinkin elfs an dressed all swell an honks
"free hundrid pounds! free hundrid pounds!" an plonks
a bunch of spons in fronter me; they shot
the lectric shandy-leer an then they arst

who wants to go to Laddins Cave an get
their bludge, an everyone says MeMeMe
an Beaunes holds up a jar es kept an light
come out of it like angels flying bright
an glimmrin round the walls an winders.' Hickee
smoked up slow and wondrous. Blinks of sweat

ducked down Bourne's flushface. 'An there was men
what dug up night an day an tuff as poke
an some what deals an them three never knows me,'
– Bourne breathed hard and fidget – 'an they chose me
cos I never ad no frens.' Ashsmoke
curled the moonlight balks. Doll gulped, 'An then

we rid away an I was glad.' The moon
hogged the other window, sulphur-bare.
Bourne wiped his head. 'An when we seen the sea
they dun our eyes up.' 'Holy shit.' The bougie
jibbled ghosts. 'An next day we was there.'
Bellbird Bogs got light: the Strike Saloon

washed-out wood and peaky bright: Doll sagged,
dough-fagged and dreary. Bourne rigged up his hat
and veil. Hickee smoked his pipe. Spring
and day squeezed the sod and every bush-thing
teemed and twittered. 'Jeez.' Bourne squirmed and spat,
mired in winter heart-night. Bellbirds zig-zagged

watery sunshafts, blank on hope. 'Free years
we digged for sixteen jars an then we said
we's goin ome, an right that night ker-*ash*
big bastard tree come whistlin down an *splash*
I buckets down the river on me ead
an there were goldbits comin out me ears

an then the water osed me eart an *whoosh*
I's gorn. I fetched up arf way down the ill,
I eard em shout in one ear an the Bay
swooshin in the tother an I lay
all day all fuller water dun an still
an when I sees the moon come up the bush

I creeps back clattrin up them knobbled stones
all pukin water.' Bourne stood up: his greasy
muslin, sick in sunshine, puffed. He reached
across a sunbeam. 'Gowon.' Kakas screeched.
'I found em; they was talkin. It were easy.
I eard em sayin sumfing, Squit and Beaunes.'

He turned his sunken freckle-face and spied
the shadows. Halo-dazzled squares of spring-glim
fizzed suspended through the walls. 'I eard –
I eard –' Bourne squinted down the lightfall. Bellbird
Bogs lit up its deadfresh hope. 'They killed im,
din they?' Hickee budged the door. Outside

the jangling green mechanicals tried
their human hearts. Doll went watery. 'Yiss.'
'They told me ee were drarned.' 'They shot im.' 'Shit.'
They dug him up, all turban-tented, split
from ear to ear. The church-roof scraped, creekhiss
on and on and on. They perched beside

new-pickaxed dirt and watched the worms. Bourne said,
'There was goldflecks on is ands.' 'Ee keeped
the jars.' Doll spat. Clods pittered in the sun.
'Where's Squit?' 'Ee chased em: there were never no one.'
Bourne puffed smoke. The raw plot oozed. They heaped
the end with stonestacks. 'God save them what's dead,'

said Bourne. 'Ay-men,' said Doll. They trudged up Bank Street,
orange-blurred. 'I seen im; waitin; there.'
Doll stopped; he pointed. 'Sittin on is brownie.'
Redlight ebbed, slipping up the bushsea,
branches, treetops, hillhigh, flickering sweetair,
gone. Doll gawped at Bourne. The seesaw dustsheet

sailed through twilight. Shreiking birds went quiet.
'How jew know,' said Doll, 'oo Squit were?' Night
shut round them like a box. 'I were you,'
said Bourne, 'before you was.' A Shining Cuckoo
flitted moonstraight; all the world half light
and spring-shoved. 'What jew mean?' said Doll. 'Shit,'

said Bourne; 'I tell you what.' He limped inside.
Doll and Hickee waited: stars that saw
the sea saw Bank Street pricked in years of bush.
The creek gabbled; crackled lightbulbs. Whoosh!
Glared up in tilley mantel-shine, Bourne tore
his blanket-bib in half and peeled the cock-tied

bandages and raised the hissing lamp
whose dazzling eyeball squealed wax-wriggled skin
all weeping sap. 'Look what they done to me.'
The moon went down. Doll ran cold. Hickee
snivelled stifle-soft. The hog tarpaulin
billowed. Bellbird Bogs soured in dawndamp.

'I member it was twilight when they come.
They rid along,' Bourne sucked a dust-cigar,
'all brave an jangled Ope all down the road.'
He hoicked and spat a sunbeam. 'Shit. I knowed
it's gold. I follered em up Dawsons Bar.
They shouts me swaller.' Doll gaped, dopey-dumb

with repetition. Bourne seesawed his chair.
'Me an Carey come from chopping tote
in Maimai. Carey said ee knew this place
an told em what . . .' He wiped his putty face.
'An . . . shit: they bought me for a Russia-coat.
It wored away.' He sniffed. The window sunsquare

glided through the floor. 'Gowon, gowon,'
said Doll. 'We rid down Broadway click as cats,'
he squashed his stub, 'an come down sowf to Blackstump.
We come through ere: I member thumpthumpthump
them crushers stampin – cross the speargrass flats
an through the ills an found the sea what shone

like meltin gold across the world. I member
ow I never been so appy. Shit.'
He gandered Doll, his hoodmilk eyes half hung
and glum. 'I member how them tuis sung
an all the poss'ble sky.' He wheezed. 'An Squit
reins me blindfold up the ill.' A blur

of springstretch sun lit up Doll's trap. 'We spade
an undrid spills an races, jack an undrid
dams an sluices, watch an undrid days
of water sprinklin gold; an Robbie weighs
is slabbies till ee rates three undrid quid
an Beaunes says let's go ome. Hot shit. We stayed

one more night. Squit brung out is whisky.
I member ow the moon were full an fat
like cheese. I woked an stuck me ead out. Moonlight
swolled the tent an all the tilts run bright.
Carey's snorin piglet-sweet.' He spat.
'I seen em underneaf a cabbage-tree:

Beaunes and Squit suspicious. They was whisprin
an the tree was too. Squit whistles free times
bellbird-like an Piggin come from Robbie's
tent all pussy-prowlin, then I sees
the iron glintin. Squit an Piggin climbs
the mullock-bank. Ee waits. I ducks me ead in.

Grunch grunch I ears is footsteps stompin
nearer nearer. "Drew! Drew!" ee spits,
"Drew! They're gawn! You member what I said!
Your orse is ready!"' Bourne upraised his head
and caught the cruellest sun. 'They all ad secrets.
Drew came straightaways. I eard them clompin

down the scree. Then nuffing. Just the wind.
I member Carey whifflin through the moonbeams.
Bags of birds blew up an it the sky
from every tree an for I works out why
its *Bang*, an I knew Drew were dead.' Streams
of daylight nailed the knotsap floor and pinned

his smelted body in its spring. 'Gowon!'
said Doll. 'Gowon.' The big white skull rolled round
and spied up squares of hope. 'I eard an orse.
One orse.' Doll gnawed his quicks and panted. 'Course
we never ad no shots; ee never found
them murderin goldspooks. Shit. An ee were gone

for ages chasin shadders through the bush,
an there were no one. Squit says all the gold
were gone. We packs our fings an rides away.
I member ow it rained up Codders Bay
like all the world were tacks an I were cold
without me Russia-coat.' The sparkle-swoosh

of Hopeful Creek went on and on. 'We come back
through the Cloudy Clear an Beaunes come too.
One night we sees this weenie light.' He stopped
and puffed. 'I member ow the tree-eads dropped
all deep an dark. I fink ee knew I knew:
it weren't that much to know. An Robbie's ack

paddered round the edge like sumfing wrong
were down there, then we flys down through the rip
an dogs all howlin. Squit goes up an knocks.
I fort I'se safe.' Bourne slipped out his matchbox:
splinters scuttled sunlit. Wip wip wip,
a robin looped in springspray whizzed along

the white verandah shocked with sun, and clicked
the rails. They watched it twit the new-move world.
'Gowon.' 'Next mornin, Piggin, Beaunes an Squit
rides off for ere to fetch the law.' He lit
another Greens cigar and brownreek swirled
the warm wood bowing beams and blew. Doll cricked

his knuckles bone by bone. 'Me an Carey
sleeped in bits all day. I fort they's gone.
I never fort –' Bourne stood up and gagged.
'Ha,' said Hickee. 'Shit.' The robin zig-zagged
roofs and fused away: the bush-crown shone
all flittered lime and glassed the blue with airy

throb. 'I eard em comin.' Bourne swung
the darkside door. 'They burned us.' Boiling white,
he stamped outside. 'In Hell like this.' The sun
flogged his face down Bank Street: springsparks spun
off twist-tin, spit-glass, juiceleaf and the leapbright
creek. He gulped the bush: darktops hung

dead shade around his botch: black to black.
The Nugget Bar in Blackstump fugged with rank:
like shot birds Squit's wersh squeals squirmed round the clink
and barrell-organ bray all piped with drink
and flush. Beaunes gasped cigars with blurry swank
and Piggin slugged a tharsend parnds. The track

up Beadys Pass lit mud-and-plank: the moon
picked blaze-swipes through the bush and all the squash
from Bellbird Bogs round-traipsed its mill. 'I woked
all skinned an blind. I member I were choked
with blister-sap.' He spat. The sunny splosh
of next week's hope bedewed the afternoon.

Hickee, Doll and Bourne steamed in the grass:
the stamper hung. 'They drarned the ol man too
oo gave us stay. Is orse come back. I rid ere
like a bag of spit an laid a year
upstairs in Hickee's snug.' Buoyed in blue,
the sun went round his skin. Up Beadys Pass

34

the souls that saved him dug like ants and pressed
the hillside full of engines through their dreams.
'I weren't allowed the light; an when I'se well
I done the dishes in the dark.' The smell
of warmpine topped the air and lapping spillstreams
drowsed them hot and hid their summer rest.

Doll fiddled with the sungrass. Bourne rolled back.
'Shake ands.' They did. Summer blazed and died.
Round-drops plocked the white verandah, splashed
the glass; booming treeshock; lightning flashed
through slewing stooks of leaves. They mouthed inside
by waxbend gleam. Twenty rooms bare-black.

And when the firstfall snow drip-tipped the town
they clopped up Bank Street, turned blow_north and brushed
through cold bush up and up. The birdman's drag-nag
hauled hoofshaky packed-up zig by zag,
ice-eyed, then Bourne, then Doll, then Hickee slushed
in bag-boots on and on and upside-down

their Brocken shapes slipped haloed through the slop.
They inched with pinprick purpose dark along
the black earth's crinkled face, their tiny trail
intent from night to night. Aloof and pale,
the moon hung, silent-still. The spookflung song
of bellbirds lulled in space. They reached the top

of Hunger Saddle: drawn grey-layered scudclouds
orange-stained; shakes of snow; scree-steeps
squeezed in sulphur-lichen. Down they cracked.
Days and nights changed colour; shingle clacked;
splotchy hail. They crossed Stump Creek. Heaps
of frozen mullock dammed the bank in shrouds

of deadpan snow. Below, the rooves of Blackstump
wet and still, dark-pooled in stands of rimu.
'Shit,' said Bourne. 'I'se goin down.' He wrapped
his oilhood tight, legged up the nag and slapped
through cold stiff bracken down to town. Two blue
rakedogs barked and bristled: thump thump thump,

he heard his heart remind him. Empty cartways,
dripdim shacks and rattling rooftins. Treespill
splashed him, slung by blows of wind. He slopped
from tent to rain-slumped tent. Blackstump stopped.
A frozen tin hand pointed up the hill:
BEADYS PASS. He spat. A redpaint blaze

wet like woundblood broke him through the bush.
He started up. The plankholds boomed. He heard
rain pelting somewhere. Pumps of horsebreath. Cut
by glistening cut he threaded trees. A hut
in bitter sunlight topped the saddle blurred
in rainbow-falling spray. He heard the swoosh

of slewing hoses, hitched his oilhood tight
and cleared the top. Drizzle-dazzled, cold
and gingered, Bourne stared through a bubbling gush
and watched a hundred squirtshine rollers flush
the hillside down the hill. Flicks of gold
winked in sudden sluices and the fanbright

irridescence arched all blinks, and hatheads
bobbed and shimmered gloss like fish. He softly
rode the ridge: a hand, a boot, a nose
he knew. He slithered through the gangs: a hose
bucked and twisted. Then he saw them: three
glittery oilskins hunched round riffle-beds

all over-surged with sludge. He splish-splashed by.
Beaunes looked up: his doused cigar bent-bit
between his teeth. He took it out. He frowned.
He poked Squit's steamy jib: Squit turned around.
His half-boiled eye jerked up at Bourne. Shit –
go on, go on. He passed the sluice. The sky

broke soft in golden seams: spread out below
he watched the tiny mudgleam antheaps washed
with rainbows. Bourne rode out. 'They're ere.' Doll spat.
'Hup-hup.' Leafcupped rain fell pitapat
and cracked in hooded ears like spades. They sploshed
across Stump Creek. Bootnicks stamped the snow.

They stopped two miles from Blackstump; strung the tent
and bushed it up with branches. Moonlight dripped
the Nugget Bar and rust-tin roof all fug
and fast-forget. 'I seen a fuckin slug,'
Squit whispered reek at Beaunes. Beanes puffed and tipped
his chair a little back. A red face leant

across the next spud-table: bug-eyes baited:
look! Unwrapped a plug of paper. Sssssh.
The bug-eyes blinked; swig-pots clonked; the red face
nodded. Beaunes tipped round: 'I know this place . . .'
Hickee guarded dawn. He heard the swish
of snowlumps brushed off trees; hoofbumps. He waited

breath-hold stiff: icewet branches clicked.
Riders snapped the bush: Piggin, Beaunes,
Bugeyes, Redface, Squit, packhorse, two.
Wordless, careful, close. They stopped. Squit blew
his fingers. Sssssss. They listened. Snowdull dregstones
rattled off their heaps. Then still. They kicked

their horses on and threaded trunks and melted
south, a bird of Beaunes' cigar-smoke wisp-bright
backwards shone off by the sky. They followed,
wetsteps holed before them while it snowed
from frozen yellow scudslabs. Day and night
they hoofed the hoofsquelch boot by boot. It pelted

sleetnails, rainslap: high on hills they saw
their tiny quarry riding: gullies piped
some sudden freak-far words beside their ears:
cold creeks kept their ripples; wetwool smears
dully marked the mosswrapped trunks and wiped
a trail of soggy blazes through the bushfloor,

thudding like a shaky where they went.
On and on, outnumbered, numb and brainstorm
tides of dead, hope-knuckled branches, grey
and cold and endless root-and-skyscratch, so they
doubted it was welcome to be warm.
Hunger Saddle. Soon they saw them, bent

against the wind and inching over baretopped
boulders, creeping through a null, white sky.
Then in their turn they cracked the tussock-height
beneath the first near glint of stars whose light
looked closer-kind than company. And high
beyond, the moon like frozen milk. They stopped.

Doll gaped up: their icy little shadows
fierce and runty. On and on and on,
more south, more east. At Fleabite Falls Squit
dug up his frozen dump: the Muir & Pippit
glimmered in an oilbag. Spring grass shone
amongst crack-dribbling white. The creeks unfroze.

They rode through drizzled bush whose warmfreed drip
sparkled round their shoulders. Then the sea:
dazzled high in mist it broke and broke
on rockheads, cracked, blew up and glittered sudsmoke,
coloured, frothed, withdrew and rose. Hickee
slithered down: he saw them clip clop clip

along the sand, their deepsqueezed hoofprints welled
with surfsheets. Tight between the waves and shorestacks
Piggin led them, slow on yellow, round
the bay and out of sight. Gannets wound
beyond the spray and dived: whistling blackbacks.
Doll and Bourne slushed down. Titis yelled.

They stood together gasping space so quickly
opened on them: Hope too far and cold
with sweat. They rested hunched on rocks and watched
the further baybend. Nothing. Redness blotched
the grey horizon: orange, yellow, gold,
withdrawing, gone. The empty sky and sea

blacked to air and whispers and the star-stitch
climbing silent-slow. Their purpose died
in everything and kept their purpose keen.
'Look,' gasped Doll. He poked the night. 'I seen –
juss there – I seen em.' 'Where?' His finger lied.
They squinnied. 'There.' A tiny, swimming firetwitch

wobbled hung in dark. 'Come on.' They crossed
the rockspit. Cliffclods pattered. Shush. Between
the waves and pungas stretched a shingle shore
that clitter-clattered tired with tides. They saw
the fire, a floating goldball looped glass-green,
sail closer, closer. Shit. They stopped, lost

in ebbs and flows of graspless black. 'Wait ere.'
Flat-cut silhouettes before the blaze;
tents put up; soft smokewhiffs; laughs. Bourne leant
against a treetrunk. Kindling cracked and sent
a spout of sparks all prickling through the smaze.
He stared. Tears snaked his meltface. He could hear

Beaunes hissing: gold gold gold, the moon and fire.
He turned away and on and on the next day
and the next they tagged their trail: each night
they caught them, beaconed by their hovering hotlight.
Doll spied through the trees. At Sweedies Bay
they upped the zigzag screebanks, scrabbling higher

scratched through new manuka round the swoosh
of three-lined swellcreeks up to bouldered sills
like bubbled tin humpgiants, lichen-haired.
Between the globegrey masses flame-wags flared
and cold reflected. Rimu piled the hills
in darkvast stooks half-flooded by the bush.

They watched them run the tents and tramp the streams.
Bugeyes dug out pools and Redface shored
a hundred trickle-tracks and jacked step-courses
still and sideruns past the banks. The horses
nosed warm rock: blue dogs squirmed and jawed
their mouths with sunshine. Crouched at glassy gleams

on smoothswirl water, Piggin, Squit and Beaunes,
one creekflood each, reeled round their pans and gawked
all spellbound while the sun wound overhead
and pricked with sheeny glint the stippled thread
of slabbies in the sludge. By dark they walked
in whispers through the rimus and the stones.

Weeks went by. Bourne and Doll by turns
spied out the camp: three tents pinched up between
round-shadowed steeps. Hickee led the nag '
down Sweedies Bay along the clattered zigzag
screebanks, where it shivered in the bluegreen
shallows sacked with fish: shore-fringe ferns

all arm-to-arm flickflacked behind. Squit
dipped his shirt – his moonlight gun – he slid
two shots. Doll watched. They mooched. They dozed. They rolled
their moonring pans and Redface weighed the gold
and locked it mostly in his snaps and hid
a crack percentage in his watchback. 'Shit,

we got enough.' Redface smiled, his beard
abristle, orange-crisp. Bugeyes beamed.
Beaunes' black words came ironing through the trees:
'We's goin ome.' Squit grinned. A warmstink breeze
like luck rubbed up the bush. Red fire-stings gleamed
and flitted out. Bourne looked at Doll. They peered

together leafspooked past the smoke. Beaunes turned
a crock of whisky. Darkness pressed: the firelight
sparked with puff. 'Come on!' They tiptoed round
the bushskirt, crossed the creeks, the slipping screeground
plocked. They stopped. Redbeard said goodnight
and swagged his beard to bed. The crackblaze burned

all hectic-red. Bugeyes wobbled up.
'When I gets ome –' he goggled at the stars.
'Oh shit.' He slumped all smiles to earth; the sparks
squibbed goldpins in his eyes. He snorted. Dogbarks
snapped the blank. 'Whazzat?' A blot of kakas
fladdered from the treetops. Bugeyes' tincup

binged the rocks – a gun! half gut-thought drawn!
They saw him see. He reeled away three creeks
and ducked by boulders through his tent. His heart
whumped: he stuck. The flyflaps lazed apart:
a seaweed breeze. The moon sailed by through streaks
of summer scud. He halfheard Redface yawn.

He saw them coming, rattling moonwash stones
as white as eggs. He tried to squeal: nothing
did. Closer closer. Squit tramped out.
Oh shit oh shit. He halfheard Redface shout
and *Blam!* The shovel! Shit! He ripped the flapfling.
Bloodred lichen dripped. He charged. Beaunes

stood blacktall, weighting Bugeyes' shovel. Hell.
'Yerarfter this?' He rammed his little claghaired
head towards them eyes. Beaunes slogged the flat:
it blanged on Bugeyes' ear. He dropped. He spat
a gummy mess. 'Youse bastard, I ain't scared –'
'Shit, you ain't nuffing.' *Whang.* Bugeyes fell

and went out with a grunt. Doll and Bourne
stared with shaky shock while Squit and Piggin
dragged the stiffs and roped them round the nags.
Beaunes tore up the tent: two saddlebags,
a hook, three goldfleck snaps, an empty weigh-tin.
Skull and Cutlass bit at blood. Dawn

dragged sweet Hope back through the sky all new.
'This aint enough,' Beaunes jangled. 'Lying cunt.'
He slit his chequered woolshirt, hacked his breeks
and yanked his boots off. Rimus gazed: the three creeks
skeltered down. Something slipped: the watchfront
flickered whitely wet. 'Less go.' Bright blue

sky and sea: they zigzagged quiet down
to Sweedies Bay and dug a hole beneath
a roof of pungas. Squit cut down the dead:
Bugeyes closed; white fat fuzzed gold-red.
Bright hurled waves; handclutch; skew-wiff teeth.
Piggin stared: the dumb-ditch rotten brown.

They rode across the mull and watched him roll
them in, and turned away, the dogs behind.
They rose and drowned in bush. The sea crashed in
and flung its froth against his back: Piggin
earthed them up. He twitched. The sun looked blind
and white. He watched each waveburst. Bourne and Doll

flicked fast stiff-shallow ferns towards the sand
and out on tiny whiteshells' prick and snap.
A horse slobbered. Piggin rocked around.
Gravetrees creaked. He spat. The low clouds wound
away behind his back. Slap . . . slap . . .
he hung on twenty lonely waves, his spadehand

lumpvein tight. And one was blackly veiled,
the other thin as flax. The sky was blue
like sweet-glass, nightmare clear and numb. They stopped.
'Shit: we ain't done,' the dark one said. He dropped
the shovel. Fuck. 'You member Robbie Drew?
We's the ones what shot im.' Piggin paled

and licked his lips. They raked him in the sea
and pushed him under. Gannets garked and wheeped.
Bubbles rode the sparkling tide and swirled
their coats. The salt horizon cut the world
in half. Bourne crouched before the tide. Doll heaped
the grave with stones and driftwood. 'Look.' Hickee

scribbled up his hat before the headland,
insect-small. 'They's stopped.' Within the green,
hot canopy of bushbloom Beaunes and Squit
sat watching, listening, horses shiffling. 'Shit:
where is ee?' Beaunes let out his teeth. 'I ain't seen –'
'Shush!' Long purple shadow-poles. Squit's hand

squeered down the bloodwarm thread inside his shirt
and cocked the Muir & Pippit, hoicked and spat.
Beaunes flung out his stale cigar: 'Go geddim.
I ain't waitin.' Bracken khaki-dim,
manuka hiss. He smiled and watched Squit's hat
swing down the bush, hold up, and careful skirt

the ferny edge. He kneed out Easy Blodstett's
spyglass: shady Squit, the grave all – fuck!
Dark dried footsteps punched the beach: something
pitched like seal-back round the swell and swing
of darkling waves. He watched Squit watch the seasuck
bleach the sand and sunset silhouettes

of treetop crowns cut through the flush. By lastlight
murk he caught how Squit looked up and picked
straight at him through the glass and reached in through
his heart and turned and – gone! Drew-drew, drew-drew,
the gloombirds piped. He stowed the snaps and kicked
the froth-nag past the treetrunks and the night.

Squit zigzagged up the bush and sidled back
and poked the Muir & Pippit through the trees:
they sailed like ships and tricked a thousand views.
Two packnags browsed; soft pigeon thruffs and coos
all dampered green; pohutukawa breeze;
far sweet waveswish soughed the time. Crack.

Whazzat? Crack. 'Beaunes? Oo's there?' The nightcloth spread.
Oosthere oosthere, the darkest tree-gaps blew
like hallways. 'We ain't Beaunes.' Squit shot the words.
His pus-eye flicked at airstripes; ringing bellbirds
flittered dark, high nectar. Squit spat: 'Oo – ?'
'You member Easy Blodstett?' 'Shit, ee's dead.'

'We's the ones what shot im.' Squit tripped back.
'What fuckwit trick – ?' They hung him in the tree,
with all the brightred flowerpins starred with gold.
He jerked the pollen down. The night went cold.
Doll sat and gnawed his nails and watched the bushsea
drown. Bourne dug the hole. Black black black.

Hickee caught Beaunes' horse half-dead next day,
its eye inkblue, its tongue blown pink. He slashed
a clap-dark blaze and cracked on up. Ridgespines
bareback hung from top to top where white pines
laved at screes and slopes. Thunder crashed
the first blobbed rain. He turned his nag away

and tagged Beaunes' wee stampede and slit a trail
in woodfresh wounds for Doll and Bourne. Seaspray
fizzed Beaunes' face and blew him hope. He blundered
down from trunk to trunk, slap-bracken slid
between the masts and peered at – Codders Bay.
Blood gobbed along his hands. He watched a fantail

flit the cliff and stay in air. How sweet
the eye-lit ocean, there, where rainblurred sun
slipped light because it was not here and gleamed
retreat, another's flood. The sink-spot seemed
all gold. The steep edge beetled, dampclods spun
dust-spraying, falling, shit. He clutched. His feet

scrabbled. Down they came towards him dark,
their hats a little glinty with the rain.
'You member me?' said Doll. 'I member you.
This ere's Ickee.' Creeeeak, the cliffy piupiu
sponge-crack roots pugged outwards; dripping bloodstain.
'You ain't shit.' He gobbed. Bourne slashed a beechbark,

wounded, seeping yellow: 'An I'se Cack.
Look what you done to me.' Stick-stain he ripped
the veil from off his hatbrim. 'You look *good*.'
Beaunes lit his teeth: Bourne bent near. The softwood
snapped and glittered. 'I got gold.' He slipped.
Bourne stamped his bloody fists. He fell. Ironblack

shoreline chilled in spindrift, flicked with gold.
Matches. Broken snaps' dead mouths all filled
by moonlight. Sandsunk whisky. Spilt cigars.
A comb. Sky still blind still pricked with stars.
Bourne looked out: swoops of kawau spilled
from cliff to cloud. Doll watched the waves. 'I'se cold.'

They crossed the hills and creeks and summer burned
the speargrass plain. They swished through toi-toi thickets
golden white and stopped, the sun direct
above. Plume-top bellbirds swayed and pecked
at softhot fronds. The horses snuffled. Tomtits
weedled airwarm through the stalks. Bourne turned

away and shivered. 'Shit. I gotta go.'
His lumpwet face half-looked. Cicadas whirred.
Doll half-waved. Toi-tois frothed and buzzed.
Heat bent the air like melted glass and muzzed
the busy world where every sprout and bird
obeyed its purpose. Doll kicked onwards slow

and Hickee followed after. Bellbird Bogs
three days away; hot-empty rooms; the creek
splish-splashing over rusty sunk máchines
and slopes of daisies bobbed the floor of Greens
Hotel; the cracked electric lightbulbs' squeak
echoed the waiting whines of two blue dogs.

*

1

A camels that trots are unique rather than are moderate
when moving because the species they generally paces only at speed.

2

Jesus where the anchor scrapes blue stones;
another place; grass that smells like lime.

3

Thisistheveryspotwherewe
escapedtogetherintothesea.

4

The rattle of rain on corrugated iron rooves reminds me
of the rattle of rain on corrugated iron rooves.

5

Our last thoughts will not be new:
you of me and me of you.

6

Do not feed the yak in unsettled conditions,
as they are known in the weather forecast.

The Ballad of Robin Hood and the Deer

The careless earth is dark and cold,
The hanging trees are high;
The greenest hope's already old;
I never see the sky.

The sun goes up, the sun goes down
Beyond the drizzled rain:
The greenest shoot's already brown;
My heart is wrapt with pain.

The thicket clicks, the bushes crack,
The wood-wind pipes and moans.
I never sleep. The sedge is black,
And death disturbs the stones.

The ghost of someone else's day
Flicked the branches white:
He snapped his study, turned away,
And guttered through the light.

The forest raised its dazzled head,
The sod ran cold and clear;
And through the glimmer, rippled red,
He saw the running deer.

Its eye was bright with silver spleen,
He smelt its cudded breath;
It studdered on the naked green,
All rigged and trimmed for death.

A livid froth beslummed its hide,
It sniffed the bitter breeze:
It cocked its puzzled head and cried
Against the fading trees.

He tracked the blaze in soft pursuit,
But something stayed its flight:
Tired of being the hunted brute,
It faced him in the light.

Its antlers shook like flaming spills,
Its eye was black as coal:
God forgive the man who kills
The master of his soul.

He set his shaft and bent his bow,
And levelled through the shade:
It panted in the bloody glow
All fixed and unafraid.

He shot: it hit. The sun went down.
It died without a sound:
And like a tower its crumpled crown
Thundered to the ground.

The sun goes up, the sun goes down
Beyond the drizzled rain:
The greenest shoot's already brown;
My heart is wrapt with pain.

The moon arose in threads of mist,
The earth was blurred with blood:
The ghostly treetops bucked and hissed;
The roots were dammed with mud.

He knelt beside his fallen hart
And stripped it of its hide:
He slit the quartered breast apart
And snapped the ribs aside.

He split the chine and sliced the paunch,
And slashed the flanks away:
He flayed the sides and freed the haunch.
The heart was cold and grey.

He cut it with a drizzled cross.
The guts were blue and bare.
Spiders stalked the bloody moss
And death was everywhere.

The thicket stirs, the branches spark;
He snatches up his knife.
Footsteps drum the rotted dark;
The forest comes to life.

The oaks rise up like castle walls,
The beech like glinting spears;
The badger thumps, the raven calls,
And whispers rack his ears.

The branches slit the livid night,
The bracken snaps – and then,
Through the misty, moonstruck light,
He sees the metal men.

The thicket clicks, the bushes crack,
The wood-wind pipes and moans.
I never sleep. The sedge is black,
And death disturbs the stones.

Their eyes are bright with silver spleen;
He smells their mutton breath:
He studders on the oozing green
All rigged and trimmed for death.

Amidst the ropes of curdled brume
They struggle with their prey:
Their glittered helmets warp the gloom.
He throws his knife away.

The wormwood smokes, the wood-owls hoot;
They slash him to the ground:
Tired of being the hunted brute,
He falls without a sound.

And all the world is hushed and awed,
And all the night is calm:
And nothing that has touched the Lord
Can come to any harm.

His fingers pluck the knotted roots,
His heart is in its grave;
His fever snaps the tender shoots.
Enough of being brave.

The careless earth is dark and cold,
The hanging trees are high:
The greenest hope's already old.
I never see the sky.

*

Christmas Message from the Vatican
received through an Iron

thump   fizz   swish   swish
like honeymoonous S.S. *Luna*
thump   Sunday's blinklit iron bow
smooths rough Adriatic bedsheet blues

all blotting calm. 'I viiish . . . I viiish . . .'
SaintOh crick-crack SaintFizz   bang
whoosh   it hisses steamholed hull capsize
'I viiish . . . I . . .'   soleplate sprayshot prayers diffuse

in rowsofeight cloud-pillars   squish
the heatknob winking   'peeez . . . peeez . . .'
wee wavelengths tremble flickerflash alight
theoops theouch theangelstatic news

roundandround the whitewalls   whish
and 'peez . . . peez . . .'   the seasheets blow
and wrap in holidays the aery-comb
and tiny *snap*!   sweet *Luna*'s   wirefire fuse.

*

4   3s

1
Water is not stored
in a camel's hump: it is
merely slowly lost.

2
eye flu
threw blew
two yew

3
Some people say that Paradise is out there somewhere.
Rubbish.
If it were, we would have found it by now.

4
Mustafa Izzet:
the blue tongue of a curled wave
rattling the shingle.

*

Brancaster Sands in the Fog

I pedalled mad out sssss across the beach
like Skoblikova sliced on speed: I hit
the highest tide in umpteen years disguised
like fog and bogged amidst the milky hush.

How small the world was. Through the whispered rush
my unseen ankles sailed, reversed, capsized
and sank. The sun played Blind-Man's-Buff. A gannet
whistled through my wheels. I felt the screech

of skuas shoot too close. I tried to say
my name, address and favourite crisps, my height
and Abbey National Number; then I fought
the falling tide of made-up facts that held

the horrors down, or had till now. Compelled
by no compulsion, loosed by brakes and caught
in unaccustomed space, a fizz of fright
frothed my happy certainties away

and left me in a one-foot bubble, staring
at my saddle. Ghosts of kittiwakes
slipped along my handlebars. The darklight
rippled. Go. Go on. The bubble followed.

Stop. Go on. Perhaps. My wee world, hollowed
out of phantom truths, oppressed me, bright
and self-reflecting. Stop. I got the shakes.
Abandon ship. They had. The last despairing

remnant of my sellotaping sense
went overboard. If I've got a soul
I didn't find it then: just my heart,
bobbing with involuntary haste.

The bike-chain cricked and cracked. What a waste.
My triumph. Is this all there is? A start:
a stop? A boat in some shushed row's control,
blown from skin to skin? The Golf Club fence

attacked my tyres and buzzed. The greens were grey.
The orange carpark wobbled through my spokes.
Sunshine slapped the reeds. Lit with sweat,
I zipped between the marshes. Someone's dog

barked behind the bungalows. The fog
tore a little. Sweet distractions. Wet
and well I hit the village shop: two Cokes,
two Double Crunches (Plain). I bowled away.

*

'The Woods of Middle England Shine . . .'

The woods of Middle England shine,
their lime-green, dappled boughs entwine

in canopies of watery light.
The sky is still and blue and bright.

Bombers leave. A summer haze
hangs along the motorways.

Underneath an ancient oak
mice in waistcoats snooze and smoke.

Bless this House. Communal bees
skim the purple Judas trees.

Lateness comes: the greenwood cools.
Water-boatmen ply the pools.

Darkness runs its Rolls around
the earth, and parks without a sound.

*

5   4s

1

I snooze aprop a punga tree
what has a longer life than me,
outwoollied midst a bloom of sheep
and tufts of light disturb my sleep.

2

I wish I was a wag again,
all double-dog and half the pain;
flying, lying, fucked and pissed
and damned for decking what I missed.

3

I see yon dogeared poppy skite;
blue mountaintops belayed with night:
I think us half-time worms work worst;
they bust too soon, or we bust first.

4

I could have been a humpey-Jack
and schoonered salt to Qom and back:
I peddle T.E. Xerox sand
with seasick sailors blue for land.

5

I think of weeds in Hooley's Suck
and dry of soul unsink my luck:
beery round the wrackless sea
I breaststroke at eternity.

*

The Ballad of Santo Caserio

Would you walk twenty miles and stab
the President of France?
I'd rather have a dog kebab
and give him one more chance.

But sometimes when the stars are bright
I think we should be good:
and then I'd probly walk all night
and then I spose I would.

Cos you can dodge the bugaboo
and quit without a fight,
or get your arse to Timbuktoo
and serve the bastards right.

Santo's little life began
in Motta-Whatta-Hole:
papa was a ferryman,
mama rowed her soul.

Some say that we are born with hope,
some say it's education;
I say it's a slippery slope
from Dinkies to Damnation.

He walked the Lamb at Passiontide
with vacuum-packed perfection;
half the bloody village cried
and missed the Resurrection.

Round the fields of boring places
sprout the seeds of pain;
sown amidst a million faces
Conscience grows in vain.

Santo made his First Communion
then his last goodbyes;
The Milanesi Bakers' Union
put him into Pies.

He read the argy-bargy books
that stirred up revolution;
he whisked up Rights with pastrycooks
and stuffed the Constitution.

It takes a heap of energy
to give ideals to others;
me, I'd rather wait and see
and do with fewer Brothers.

But sometimes when the stars are bright
I think we should be good;
and then I'd probly talk all night,
and then I spose I would.

He dished up pamphlets, marched for peace
and organised disorder;
he unattacked the City Police
and slipped across the border.

He wandered here, he wandered there,
the Comrades took him in
from Val deDream to Val D'Isere,
from Trouble to Turin.

'Dear F., I've got a job in Sete.
The world will soon be free!
I haven't done the details yet.
Long Live Anarchy!'

'Dear P., The hour of vengeance nears!
Remember what I said!
The air has putrefied my ears.
I have to stay in bed.'

'Dear Comrade S., I'm nearly better.
Please give X these francs.
This will be my final letter.
Day is dawning! Thanks.'

One day he bought a ten-inch knife
and caught the train to Vienne:
I'd rather have a quiet life
and mow the lawn again.

But sometimes when the stars are bright
I think we should be good;
and then I'd probly see the light,
and then I spose I would.

He walked to Lyons. Half way there
a steam-tram partied past.
He hurried on to Guillotiere.
Night was falling fast.

He saw the lamplit Bourse ablaze,
he heard the bourgeoises shout;
trumpets blared the Marseillaise.
The Horseguards clattered out.

He struggled forward, row by row,
the escort smacked their drums.
'Monsieur le President Carnot!'
a boy yelled. 'Here he comes!'

I grabbed the knife inside my coat.
I pushed the front row back.
A hatbrim brushed across my throat.
The carriage-cloth was black.

He waved. I yanked the dagger free.
His frock-coat puffed apart.
I shouted, 'Long Live Anarchy!'
and stabbed him in the heart.

He looked his killer in the eyes
and blood seeped through his shirt;
he murmured, 'I apologise';
he whispered, 'I've been hurt.'

I spose he wasn't all that bad,
but probly bad enough;
but death is cruel and life is sad
and justice can be rough.

The population blew a fuse
and anti-Wopped the city;
me, I usually watch the news
with vegetable pity.

But sometimes when the stars are bright
I think we should be good;
and then I'd probly watch all night
and then I spose I would.

They sentenced him in record time.
He offered no defence.
'What I have done is not a crime:
only common sense.'

They tied him to his prison bed.
He turned and faced the wall.
For seven days, the warders said,
he never spoke at all.

I always bloody hate this part;
it makes me bloody sick.
I hear my fatal coward's heart;
I hope they do it quick.

And when they came at five o'clock
I shit my pants and cried;
my brain dissolved in fucking shock
and all my dreaming died.

They had to help him up the stairs;
they had to carry me.
We closed our eyes and said our prayers:
'Long Live Anarchy!'

There's right and wrong in everyone,
and every issue's grey;
life is just a bit of fun,
and then we fade away.

But sometimes when the stars are bright
I think we should be good;
and then I'd probly walk all night,
and then I spose I would.

*

The Assistant Auditor for Agriculture Visits Uzbekistan

See those porky patchwork cotton clouds
(sickbag bomp bomp) and wirebright irrig-
(green and green and) -ation, fish in tins
and pinky sponge with cream or was it? give me

strength (' -ing our descent' boing whang
zip) a zillion lemon trees ('your seat belts
when –') and palest stars unpick a blueing
blue when boorish plenty sucks the tyres.

Her hair perspired. 'Are these,' she lightly smiled,
'all peaches?' 'Yiss.' She read some curly vines
like writing looped across the land in lines
and fruit fields far away. They drove her there.

'Stop.' They stopped. She turned her glasses east
with gauzy glare. 'And who,' she aitched, 'is that?'
'Is Ali Bozh.' 'Come on.' He raised his hat.
She hoofed across while saplings whisked the blue.

(Whisper, 'What are – ?' *Epples.*') Ali Bozh
gnarled some white hello: she shook his hand.
'Is all of this,' she lightly smiled, 'your land?'
'Yiss.' He creaked. She tapped two whippy letters:

'These,' her earrings burned, 'will never fruit
before erhum you die.' His watery eyes
swerved up to Heaven: a happy host of flies
sparked round his skull. 'Dead men dug for me;

now I dig for men who are not born.'
She watched the booming sun move round his mouth.
What use was that? She turned her glasses south.
Plums plums plums. She pushed a dollar

down his barky fingers; 'Thank you.' 'Wait!
I ate because I did not die; and others
died and did not eat;' (sickbag) 'and others . . .'
twanging row by row all earth all words . . .

The blue blancmange ('No Smoking sign is off.
We hope you –') sliding off the air (your spoon)
and white and white each painted page blurs out
the doubtful sentence of its spawny lines.

See those bosky glum and sad-green pines
(bomp-bomp) and cream or was it? hauling back
some lovely neon light that glinks the tyres
('-ing our descent') and give me strength. She smiled.

*

2   5s

1

Night-time like a lift sucks up on yonder
snowy warp: by twilight's nipping glitz
I quit each col by col and up and up
an icy mile all overtakes me now
and what was furthest, fairest, finest falls.

2

Good try.
You can do better.
You have not answered the question.
Some good bits here.
Somewhat short.

*

Altoo and the Bet about God

STA.

The world is round, O brothers; Heaven flies
farflung on whizz-blue atoms; God is Great;
angels go a million miles a minute;
space gapes like a camel's yawn and in it
suns and moons and stars phlogisticate
the endless, sparkling tentage of the skies.

But man is dust upright awhile; beskinned
with clotted blood; and water salt; and earth
all over-rasped with sand; and tractors slewed
on rotted lemons; pricked with solitude
and company and thirst; and nothing worth
a Heaven-atom, broken by the wind.

And yet God loves him; Seventh Heaven streams
sufficient still; and oozy watergrapes
bright-bubbled green like walking through His veins;
and sprinklered souls; and Russian aeroplanes
whose rows of high, strobotic eyes see shapes
undreamt but in the engine of His dreams.

Make no plans without permission; take
no scrap before you ask; at every beat
your heart makes, thank Him; every little nightdeath,
pray. Who persists your bedblind slightbreath?
Who holds up your heart? O Incomplete!
Who wakes you, Thoughtless, lest you never wake?

Observation rips the nimbostratus;
down and down the optic, hurtling blue;
the world's edge; the lemon moon upturned;
the sun aswoon; the desert coffee-burned;
dust; the city; cock-a-doodle-doo!
Thursday. Altoo got up for a piss.

WOR.

The day was hot already. Someone's sheet
hung lazy from a window; Victory Block,
high-toasted concrete. Altoo poured his tea.
Lifts clunked; a hundred Bychkov Fuji
AirCool fanbelts squealed. Six o'clock.
A buzz of traffic hauled up through the heat.

He wound the window open; spicy balm-air
pricked his nose puffed up with diesel. Sunblips
pinged a hundred panes. Please God show me
where the Way is. High beyond him foamy
cloudballs stockstill in the heat. His lips
with careful slowness Oed the morning prayer.

By half past six the Egg Soup Lucky Diner
steamed with drip and clished tin plates. Altoo,
strangled in a starchwhite tightshirt, swerved
around his plastic tables, shout-and-served
the early workers; egg soup blodged like glue
from fubsy pans, and SquidBits made in China.

Then the dishes; then an Honest Cloud
beside the window. Spacious Street was booming:
bikecabs, bullcarts, buses, screws and scooters,
taxis, trashfires, thrashtyres, horses, hooters,
fruitsquash, shopshouts, sheepshit, vrooming, fuming.
Altoo picked his nose. The outglassed crowd

like pictures at the pictures danced and sang
for his reflection. Hm. Did God intend
his chicks to stamp and sweat so much to get
to Heaven? Lunchtime hog. A Russian jet
chalked the blue through evening soup. To bend
and break for goodness' sake? The backbell rang.

BET.

'Abu!' 'Altoo!' 'How was Orsk?' The sky
smudged; the blinds came down; the tilley spat.
Darkness dropped on Spacious Street. 'Today,'
said Altoo in a shrug-and-thoughtful way,
'I wondered why I worked.' He smiled. They sat
and watched the orange mantle fade and die.

'Life's too short,' said Abu, sighing smoke;
but not what for. Altoo locked the shop.
They went to Yelma's Teahouse. 'Abu! Altoo!'
'Beji!' Kettles bubbled; rows of duckblue
teacups clinked; the gentle plop-plop-plop
of teapots; fridgy-tinkling cans of Coke.

They smoked and sucked their Prarie Green. The slap
of checkers; neon buzz and Russian bop.
The amber still-time puffed away. 'I'm fucked,'
said Abu; Beji grumbled plumbing sucked.
'God is Great,' said Altoo, 'We could stop
tomorrow.' Beji slurped his saucer; 'Crap.'

Abu's eyes went hot; 'You wanna bet?'
Fridge-tins fluttered dots across the glass.
'Yes,' said Altoo, sick-excited. 'Balls,'
said Beji fishing down his overalls;
he waved his HinduKushCard; 'Kiss my arse.'
Abu leered and lit a cigarette.

'Here's the deal.' He pushed the cups away
and clicked his briefcase. *'No work for a year.*
You live in common view.' – he wrote with care –
'and God provides.' He smiled. 'I think that's fair?'
And if you do it' – Beji ordered beer –
'you get a skiing trip to Osh. I pay.'

69

BOX.

Altoo let the Diner, closed his flat
and went to Beji's. Window-boxes blared
with roses; summer stoked the last spring days.
Sandscrews spindly-poled the desert; bluejays
bleeped in dusty trees. Altoo stared
across the concrete; Abu cooed the cat.

The moon made cardboard cutouts up the walls.
Three shadows glided through the floors of Cosmos
Block with something boxy. Black-on-milk
they turned up Spacious Street. Pale-pearled like silk
the moony awnings; veggie phantoms; crisscross
bamboo tilt-sticks; ghosty market stalls.

'Right,' said Abu. 'Drop it here then.' *Crash.*
He phewed. Altoo shied a sheepish smile.
'Piss it, brother!' Beji slapped his hand.
'God be with you.' Tiny twists of sand
corkscrewed past. Altoo made a pile
of rugs and cushions. 'Cheese!' said Beji. *Flash.*

The photo poks a skinny soul in bulbspark
trainers, jeans, fake-Nike T-shirt, cap
and laser eyeballs sitting in a box;
behind him lift the lumed apartment blocks
like pastel crayons, moon-chalked; stallsheets flap
stilly. Yellow. Dazzle. Dim. Dark.

Altoo sighed. The moon peered down. A sheep
chomped a rotten cabbage. God is Great;
the Merciful, the Kind, O show me where
the Way is, King of Judgement, hear my prayer.
He punched some cushions. Time went soft. You wait:
a year is peanuts! Altoo slumped asleep.

JUN.

'Oi! Dickhead!' Altoo whoozed. The sky
had swapped the moon for sunshine. Early-birds
were clopping past; a squat-ass stacked with swedes
and onions bounced behind. They stopped. Their beads
clacked. 'You real?' They spat. They swapped some swearwords.
'Missus kick you out man?' 'Crazy guy.'

Altoo boffed the cushions: God said *Go!*
Things wound up and time wound round regardless:
then they both wound down. A half-plucked chook
rolled its tapioca-eye to look
in Altoo's box; it clip-toed through the fruitpiss
trash and roosted in a rug. A row

of melons mimicked planets in the sky,
which lay above, all palpable and numb.
Someone grilled the hen for Altoo's lunch.
The days rolled into one: sweet tea, a bunch
of chillies, Russian crisps and bubblegum
in evening's empty caravanserai.

Abu squirmed. His wife's rose-sweated hair
rewired his back. The hot-sand slopes of Osh
rushed up and clogged the throbbing chalet doors.
Bychkov Fuji AirCools drummed the floors
of Cosmos Block. She rolled and nudged him squash
against the wall. The Bank sat in a chair:

'Work and whirl!' its entrance snapped. A shit
tornado whizzed towards his nose; he sneezed
awake. The cat was honking. One month done!
The lino steamed. I bet he thinks he's won
already; Abu snarled; he writhed; he squeezed
Budaya's gorgeous works; the tight sheet split.

JUL.

One baking day a Russian jet buzzed in
perfumed with tourists: KushTours Eastern Jewels.
Cameras popped: cones of salt and saffron;
pyramids of plums and peppers shone
like shade and bowls of cheese in coldfat pools;
budgies, jeans and domes of rabbit-skin.

They snapped the mystic mystic popping grapes;
they snapped the ducks in Spacious Street; they snapped
themselves; they bounced away in Beji's jeep
towards the jewelled, snowplume peaks. A heap
of snappy bags and cases, stamped and strapped,
beseiged the moonlight box with crazy shapes.

While Altoo slept they skiied the powder steeps
with torches on their heads; and while he watched
the world go by they ploughed around the vasty
white and snapped the fearful fridge. Nasty
boils pricked his back; rashes splotched
his blotchy legs. Then he got the creeps:

they felt like he was in a huge balloon
and all the world was painted on its skin
and someone popped it. Sunlight squeezed his eyes;
his heart went *boom*; he sat in space; flies
sipped his sweat; he throbbed. The muezzin
sang God is Great like honey round the moon.

The Tour rolled in. They took their luggage back
and smiled and paid Altoo and flew away:
blushes lit the wings; a cool sun rose.
'You worked,' said Abu; Altoo shrugged; 'God knows.'
Camels clipclopped past, day by day
by day down Spacious Street. His toes went black.

AUG.

Abu stroked the cat; it arched and purr'ed.
TV flickers spooked against the wall.
Budaya giggled. Darkness filled the glass.
He scowled: wait til winter bites his arse!
Altoo squeezed his boils. A fishy birdcall
bleeped – three times – a tough, gigantic bird

tiptoed through the empty stalls; it stopped
and bleeped again. Altoo craned and peeked.
Two more; they stalked a little, rusty Peugeot
parked at Yelma's. Chisels rattled. 'Go,'
yapped Bigbird. Shining sweat, the fat one sneaked
the sleeping car. He poked. The doorlock popped.

'Get in you stupid bastard!' Fatone squashed
the driver's seat. The wee suspension screamed.
'Scaff it! Scaff it!' Crack. The engine vroomed.
Altoo megaphoned his hands and boomed,
'Freeze, punks!' They froze. The engine steamed
and jogged; headlights blinked; wipers washed

the windscreen. Lights came on down Spacious Street.
Bigbird drew his chisel. 'Make my day!'
blared Altoo. Fatone raised his hands. The moon
shot them spellbound like a searchlight. Soon
the Police rolled up and marched the birds away.
Silence overfurled the midnight heat.

Chief Inspector Xloog, all tinsel-dressed,
flashed his shades and boots. The market hushed.
'Crime,' he gleamed and goshed, 'has dropped by ten
percent' – they cheered – 'in this conblurgumen.'
He beamed; the camels gurked; Altoo flushed
with civic pride. A medal jewelled his chest.

SEP.

Misty mornings, duller days. Heat
sucked backwards like a genie through the gritty,
sailing blocks and crumpled in the sand.
Altoo lapped his lessee's soup: canned
Korean crap. His tea was stale. The pretty,
painted fruitsigns vanished. Spacious Street

groaned with bumping, thumping bags of grain
that lumped and rumbled up and down, and sacks
of furry Friendship Rice that cracked the slabs
and squashed the asphalt flat. Altoo's scabs,
unroasted, shrank. The clouds congealed like wax
and spat their first, unfriendly gobs of rain.

One night, a watchful woman, shady-veiled,
descended from a taxi near the park.
She hurried down the street beneath the drapes
of dim and bellied canvas; anxious shapes
swung behind her. Altoo dozed. The dark
hush-shadow rustled near; the halfmoon sailed

discreetly, like an eyeball. Altoo half
awoke; the cushions yawned. 'Hide this, *please!*'
'Whazzat?' She pushed a pink purse in his hand.
Altoo toppled gently back to dreamland.
Another taxi nosed the bluepark trees,
glinting at him. Ssh. A muffled laugh;

two tinkling silhouettes and tiptoe feet;
they stopped; they rummaged dainty round his box;
they flapped away. Next morning Altoo found
two stones wrapped in a message on the ground:
'Money should be spent: for hiding, rocks
are just as good.' The sun licked Spacious Street.

OCT.

Autumn zincked the desert. Heaven cooled
its energetic brow in preparation
for the forecast fiery fridge. Stars
stabbed the dark like pins. Samovars
steamed the glass with honeyed lachrymation
all along the street. Someone pulled

the Egg Soup Lucky Diner's curtains shut.
Altoo watched. Golden shadows jiggled
inside-out. The first Bychkov Hawaii
AirWarm fanbelts revved up with a sigh
of rancid dustburn. Sadly, Altoo wriggled
in his rugs and pecked a woody doughnut

while the planets orbed their orbits high
above his head, like life, too slow to see.
He sank amongst his cushions. God is Great:
the atom-crawling synchromesh of fate
revolves in Greek beyond eternity
and sparks of purpose spill across the sky.

The Diner closed. Heaven moved but stayed
the same. Yelma's glowed. Beji pinned
a late-night tap and charged the joey double.
He watched the sludge of soapshit dredge and bubble
down the plughole like his dreams. The wind
blew sand through Labour Block. The joey paid.

And suddenly a shooting star cut free
and threw its melted knot across the night.
Altoo saw it; some, though unprepared,
were lucky too; others, who had stared
at space for ages, missed it. By the light
of fading glitters Abu sucked his tea.

NOV.

The weather chilled and danked. He smiled. What care
or comfort stirs its stumps when God's great nation
snuggles round its cosy, well-earned rest?
The heating reeled with dizzy strain. The best
intentions crack with frost and botheration
breaks with beastly need. He pushed his armchair

near the stove. The cat dribbled. Spotlit
by the whitish moon, Altoo's box
floated like a spaceship. Something crashed
somewhere. Altoo stiffened. Something flashed
from wall to wall between the chilly blocks
of flats; a bottle smashed and tinkled. 'Shit.'

A shadow weaved his way. A little screw
of steamsweat swirled in spirals off its skull.
It peered at him and wobbled. Altoo smiled
politely. Plonk. It flopped and crocodiled
with all its teeth. 'Gidday.' Its eyes were dull
with milky disappointment. Timbuktoo,

it whoozed with confidential winks, was its
abiding dream; it wanted, hic, to go there
now. Altoo thought a while and said,
'Go up Spacious Street – turn left – and head
towards the HotDog Stand in Freedom Square:
then ask again.' The shadow grinned; flits

of hope lit up its eyes. 'And if you keep
on asking' – Altoo watched it find its feet –
'eventually you'll get to Timbuktoo.'
As this could not be otherwise than true,
the shadow staggered off down Spacious Street
and steamed away. Altoo went to sleep.

DEC.

Colder, barer, duller, darker, grim:
Altoo rode the world the others ditched
for counterfeited summer days, and span
in sheets of snow his patient caravan
alone. Above, the trudging stars all stitched
their same, mechanic way around the rim

of Heaven. God is Great: God is Great:
the rest just happens. Lightning axed the air.
Beji snored in Yelma's arms; the gaslamp
copper-hissed their skins still sweetly damp
and dumb. Thunder frothed their underwear
across the lino. Altoo sneezed. A plate

of lukewarm chips went pulpy at his feet;
his teapot filled with rain; he softly slubbed
in miles of frosty fog. A goat, advancing
at his sampan like Pavlova dancing
through dry-ice, awoke him. Altoo rubbed
his eyes; the muslin swirled; a plaintive bleat

echoed in the ocean. 'Wakey-wakey!'
Snowflakes fluttered. Soup and tea steamed
like hot baths; the spoon clunked his teeth;
noodles hissed. The goat yawned underneath
the rugs. Beji stamped his feet and beamed;
'Morning, brother.' Altoo wagged his shaky,

spooning hand; 'The night in s-s-silk
has passed and so ha-has the night in shit.'
He slurped his golden tea; the sugar stung
like sparks. A car coughed past. The sun hung,
a pallid, paper circle. Beji lit
an Honest Cloud; the smoke surfed out like milk.

JAN.

The old year went; the new year came. A blast
of fireworks, softly seen, chatoyanced
in Freedom Square all fizzy green and airlate
pops. The desert glittered. God is Great.
Beyond the concrete towers the revellers danced
and hooted, distance-damped, while Time slipped past

between the stars, ratted in a Russian
jet. The party faded like a liner
screwing out to sea. Altoo shivered:
cardoors, revs, shoe-crunch, ice. The livid
light of roman candles glitzed the Diner
ferried by a bottleglass percussion

bouncing like the bacchae in a line.
They sparkled past and died. Did God intend
his chicks to gobble joy so bull and brief?
A day, a drug, a dream, a dumb relief
from donkeydrudge and darkness? Is the end
of all this bustle death? Whose crap design

condemns the man and saves the mountain? Are
the heavens tiny twinklings of some fragile
fun extinguished donkey's years ago?
God knows. Altoo sneezed. Squirts of snow
dribbled down the stalls; a gobby pile
of half-chewed hotdogs blurted from a car.

It sat there like temptation; then it seemed
less tempting. Abu shaved; the Bychkov Hawaii
AirWarm fanbelts juddered; sleep glued up
his eyes; the mirror lanced with light; a cup
of hot-tap tea; Budaya yawned goodbye;
he gave the cat its Grin; the dark lift screamed.

FEB.

Winter stropped its cruellest cold. The market
shut. Altoo gobbled tins of Primrose
Bluebeans, Russian eels and LongLife Rice
With Pickled Cabbage. Scaly panes of ice
crackled in his rugweave; then his toes
went waxy-grey and sour. He tried to sit

arse-outwards, like a camel, but his ears
swelled up with thumps and all his jackjoints creaked
and cracked. He squirmed. He got the creeps again;
he saw the beating blankets of his brain
stretched between the stalls; his hearthole leaked
and Reason crackled out like chandeliers

colliding in a sandstorm. God is Great.
He saw his bed; its sponge-inviting mattress
warbled nursery-rhymes. 'Altoo!' 'Abu!'
'Shit. Give up! Go home!' Teary goo
dribbled down his eyes; a blot of piss
inked his shitstiff jeans; a shattered plate

spilled its ice-still stew. 'No, no,' he smiled.
Two steamy shadows tiptoed round the box;
Abu stripped him bare; Budaya washed
his body from a bucket; soapsuds sploshed
and blubbed; they rubbed him dry; they dressed him: socks,
longjohns, tracksuit, skihat, gloves. They piled

a tender deck of duvets round his dreams
and hurried home. The desert flipped from grey
to gold; the sun observed the swaddling lump
and slowly zoomed away. The thump-a-thump
of fanbelts bumped the blocks and Altoo lay
all mummied in the market, striped with sunbeams.

MAR.

Someone rang the paper. Winter shrank:
the last-loose ice-slops gurgled down the drain
and birds breezed back. 'Icebox Man Beats Freeze:
I Trusted God'. His photo smiled. The Chinese
House of Coats donated two Champagne
Exclusive Duck-Sport Parkas; Abu's Bank

pledged a KingSize Thermos-Flask-and-Mug
emblazoned with their logo; Lopchin's Lamplight
Lounge presented four electric blankets
plugging Lopchin's Lamplight Lounge; and Zit's
Boutique sent flowers. The days went brisk and bright.
Snug inside a Bychkov HomeSmile rug,

Altoo watched the world. He knew he'd won;
he knew that spring's abundant blossom brought
his undiscriminating plenty; soon,
egged on by the earth, his fat cocoon
would come unstuck and like a cosmonaut
loosed into Heaven, tumbling at the sun,

he'd recognise salvation by its spark.
The creeps dissolved. Redressed, refreshed, retreaded,
sucked and souped, one purple night he saw
a ten-ton Moscow Motors Dinosaur
swoosh down Spacious Street; its triple-headed
trumpets squawked; it towered towards the park

and twinked its shape in fairy-lights between
the sagging stalls and thundered off in chrome.
Abu checked his Savings Book and stroked
the cat. The desert stirred. Beji smoked
and lagered long in Yelma's, then went home.
The concrete giants warped like plasticine.

APR.

Beji downed some Cornflakes; sunlight speared
his skew pyjamas. Far beyond the blocktop
reek he watched the desert gleam. Scrunch,
scrunch, dribble, gulp. A little bunch
of bulb-blades cracked the roof of Gorby's Cakeshop.
Iceblobs dribbled, dropped and disappeared.

Yelma licked his spoon. The sky burst blue.
The market opened. Abu launched the lift
in Cosmos Block. Traffic honked and fumed.
The Diner steamed as Heaven unentombed
its sweet creation. Altoo yawned and sniffed
the promised tang from here to Timbuktoo.

'My dad says you know God.' He rubbed his eyes.
'I've got my Native Plants Exam today'.
The little glasses blinked. 'I want a A.'
The gutters gushed and gulped; she marched away.
He prayed and prayed; the sky went effish grey
and growled with zips of lightning; dragonflies

bounced and blew their briefness. Who rerights
your blurbrained hand amidst a world of tears?
O Blind! O Semi-Souled! She bustled back.
'I got a B.' She scowled. The clouds went black
and scuttled. God is Great. He flustered. Smears
of smog and mizzle murked the highblock lights.

She beamed her glasses at him. Cars burned by.
Altoo cringed. 'I spose a B will do.
Thanks for trying. Bye.' She skipped away.
He snuggled down. The last low streaks of day
ran like watercolours, pink and blue.
The desert shivered, sank, and drank the sky.

MAY.

The year rolled up. Abu booked the SnowSun
FreeSki Chalet Break for five in Osh;
Beji cleaned the jeep; Altoo sat
and watched the market fill up fresh and fat.
Camels swayed the sweetstuff in; the slosh
and slither steamed away. 'Okay, you won':

Abu waved the tickets in his face.
A honey-moon slid shining overhead;
they shared an Honest Cloud. On Labour Day
the City Council came, and went away.
Some custard dabchicks goofed across his bed
and sunshine flooded through the marketplace.

The thirty-first of May had twied its light
when Altoo faced his God alone. The sky
was starry-red and Spacious Street stood still.
Somewhere out in space His sifting will,
like camels leaving everywhere, blew high
and handsome. *Whoosh!* A Russian satellite

whisper-hissed its ghost around the earth:
hushed within, a blue strobotic lens
signalled in its vacuum, blip blip blip.
The warm wind wound; the gentle drip-drip-drip
of Altoo's thermos pricked the concrete. Cleanse
your sheepshit, swoonsick spirit! What is worth

the sacking of your soul? No quark replied.
Altoo pulled the duvet round his head
and fell asleep. The Picture Palace gleamed;
in Freedom Square a hundred hotdogs steamed;
Abu smoked; Budaya went to bed;
the Bychkov Hawaii AirWarm fanbelts sighed.

AFT.

Nurses ether-clicked along the lino.
'Doctor Phlasmagist.' His crutches clattered
insect-awkward down the whitewall ward.
She poked his gastrocnemius; hummed and hawed;
she banged his hamstrings, twanged his tendons, patted
up and down his flexors, to and fro

across his ebbed extensors. 'Exercise!
Exercise!' Each morning Altoo cranked
and bobbed and swayed around the sunswept flat;
Budaya vacuumed golden dust; the cat
backstroked round the rug; Abu banked;
Beji plumbed; the Diner dined; blue skies

blued and birded. Sap shot up the soul.
Swerving in his starchwhite tightshirt, Altoo
repossessed the Egg Soup Lucky Diner,
his plastic-table-tinplate-made-in-China-
panslob-squidfat-steamy-bonsai-bamboo-
papered-neon-heaven. Boing: a bowl

of SquidBits boiled in noodlewater. Abu
smiled. Boing: Budaya poked her fish-bog.
Boing: boing: 'Congratulations!' 'Cheese!'
said Beji. *Flash!* The photo poks a squeeze
of flushface flasheyes whoop-stopped in a fog
of scudsy steam. Cock-a-doodle-doo!

Altoo rubbed his eyes. His Spartak Moscow
HeadCase oppilated on the floor.
Five o'clock. The rooftops dozed. Beep beep!
He jangled down the lift. Beji's jeep
sat permed with skis in Victory Street; the door
stood shining open. Altoo grinned. 'Let's go!'

REW.

Powder squeaked beneath their edges; still
and dizzy perched in space; the skilift jingled
like a teaspoon far below. They scrunched,
herringbone, away. The great peaks bunched
before them, deadly bright. Altoo tingled,
gulped and slapped his boards across the chill

high rim. He chased his steamtrain breath. They crossed
the furthest ridge. They stopped. Its tranquil tension
gripped the silent mountains. Altoo stared.
Cold air sheered the light; his glasses glared.
He puffed. They gazed with rapt incomprehension
round the sky, their skihats crowned with frost.

'Come on!' said Abu. One by one they swooshed
the edge away and swooped in big slow Us
from slope to slope towards the squealing whirl.
Evening pinked the snow; a leaden swirl
numbed the mighty tops with curlicues
of darkness. God is Great. Altoo pushed

a pot of Prarie Green across the table.
The chalet danced with firelight. Yelma poured
a glassful; Beji wandered to the window.
Yellow lightsquares streaked the glassy snow;
like angel-plans the skilift pylons soared
beyond the starlit slope; the silent cable

stretched from wheel to wheel. The moon looked cold.
Beji fetched his cards; Altoo dozed;
Abu puffed an Honest Cloud; Budaya
drowsy-eyed the picture in the fire.
The tilley hissed and glimmered. Yelma closed
the curtains; all the woodwalls gleamed with gold.

FLI.

Two weeks sparkled past. They skinned up slopes
together, each one lost in sweat and smiles;
they traversed endless steepbacks, gliding still
and side by side; they crashed in every Downhill,
Slalom, Skate and Sledge; they tramped for miles
beyond the busy basin tied with ropes

and swizzled back in squeal-collapsing swoops;
they sunbathed on the chalet steps; they jived
to Igor's Yak Quartet beneath a craze
of paper lanterns. Day by day the days
dissolved, and when the rosy end arrived
they jeeped to Myk-Myk Airport. Little groups

of shivering tourists goggled at the sky.
A Khrushchyov K-5 smashed the clouds aside
and bounced to earth; its greengilled contents tiptoed
down the gangway. Next! The second airload
teetered on; propellers screamed; the pop-eyed
jetset clawed their armrests. With a cry

of *k-k-kaaaaaaargh!* the Khrushchyov clambered through
the evening clouds and, burbling, moaned towards
the setting sun. His life in other hands,
Altoo wiped the oval window; bands
of rubric fired the peaks that spiked like swords
the anaesthetic heavens. Up they flew

in gasping triumph past the utmost height
of everything on earth. Budaya wiped
her eyes and Beji blogged the sickbag. Soon
the plane plunged back to Myk-Myk past the moon,
which rose in automatic stupor, striped
with clouds of vapour, yellow, sallow, white.

FIN.

The world goes round; our faint-full dynamo
flickers then is gone; and if we keep
our promises, it is not we whose power
prevailed, but He. O Doubtful-Every-Hour!
The caravan comes home; the sea is deep
but has its end and that is all you know.

The Egg Soup Lucky Diner steamed with fug
and clished tin plates; Altoo watched the dinner
diners gulp their goo; the TV blinked
the Moscow Lotto; spoons and glasses clinked.
Altoo puffed an Honest Cloud. The winner
waved her cheque; the signal zizzed; a bluebug

blatted at the screen. The endless stir
of every life, the sleeper's heart, the germ,
the worm, the fag, the grind, the shine, the shit,
the kicks, the bud, the blood, the pricks, the fit,
the fat, the act, the thought, the sport, the sperm,
the long, relentless, beating, bloody blur

has one intent: it is not yours. The sun
went down; the desert whispered, level-red;
the concrete blocks like filling glasses gloomed
from floor to floor; the empty liftshafts boomed.
Altoo said his prayers and went to bed.
Don't ask for your salvation: it is done.

Make no plans without permission; take
no scrap before you ask; at every beat
your heart makes, thank Him; every little nightdeath,
pray. Who persists your bedblind slightbreath?
Who holds up your heart, O Incomplete?
Who wakes you, Thoughtless, lest you never wake!

*

TWOC

Alpha Schmalpha Tango Wango
Jeez, it's hot; my vinyl interior warps
like burned paper and the park is brown.

Roger Wilko blocks the sticky end
of Duncan Road. I wave my burning sleeves.
The helicopter hangs from nothing blue.

I change down and stare. Arthur Street,
Roger; Roger, Cressy Road. Their dayglo limeline
loops the melted neighbourhood, come out you are

surrounded. I stop underneath a streetlight's
insect head and ahem clean my shades. Much better:
now I see each two-way birdbleep – there –

TWOC, TWOC, TWOC: Bolter's Timber Yard,
its hot planks oozing gum: rayguns dazzle   –
from The Crown's octagonal conservatory.

Green through my wizard lenses I espy
whose green abandoned car grunt-dead
and oozy petrol slips, half-gas, away

and he who done it in the glass I see
like some hot fish swims round the great escape
yard to yard. The birdie's eye, extending,

cannot see somewhere near here
Sir Plantivere went thump and thump
his rot-bewildered nag went down

and dumped him in the tangly tents
of bogbriar, quaking grass and old bugs,
eighteen, and the pleasured smash behind him

and before and near here the raven's eye, whirring,
taped the men of England fight aarrk-aarrk
in Christendom and crap. The swamp weeps.

Blood slips out between its gnashers
oozy on the earth: I see together:
glory glory hoodlum doodlum: one,

the other; both and neither. Then I turn the key.
My mirrors show me squares of summer
and the winter deep in earth.

*

1 6

Goodnight. Climb into bed
and leave to faith
your moving parts:
laid out with the dead
and barely safe
in other hearts.

*

Fyodor the Crow

There was once a crow who got fed up
with his dozy life up the larches
in the fields on the banks of the Ulu-Yul
and decided to move his nest.

His name was Fyodor Al-Din.

The river burbled by beneath him,
the trees threw off their leaves and grew them again,
the weather changed from quite nice to bloody cold
and Fyodor gobbled anything he could get his beak on.

And that was about as exciting as it got.

'Somewhere,' said Fyodor Al-Din, pluffing his feathers
and blinking his tired little eyes at the sky,
'things have got to be better than this.'
Clouds rolled over the larches, and he sighed.

That night his wings twitched as he dreamed.

Next day, Fyodor Al-Din kicked a hole in his nest,
stuffed himself with wortleberries and mayflies
and flapped away to the west going 'Kraa-Kraa'
while keeping a hopeful eye on the world below.

The burbling of the Ulu-Yul faded away behind him.

Miles of fuzzy treetops passed beneath him,
the green and brown and yellow shapes of fields
and wrinkled hillsides like dried fish.
His little heart banged faster than rain.

At last he came to a small town called Suy'ga.

He landed on a block of flats and looked around.
The streets were full of cars and trucks.
A yellowy fog hung about the rooves.
The trees stretched up their heads and gasped.

Fyodor Al-Din blinked his little eyes and flew away.

He flapped on all through the night
against a sour wind. His lungs burned.
His little gizzard creaked with hunger.
He gobbled some sour berries and slept in a pine tree.

He hid himself in a tiny fortress of needles.

The next day, wobbly with exhaustion,
Fyodor Al-Din came to the suburbs of Cherkesovo.
He could have walked on the rooves for hours and never
reached the end. He hopped up a television aerial.

The thin sunshine dribbled palely on a row of bungalows.

Below him lay the garden of Mr and Mrs Golodin,
who worked in the office of a private towel factory.
It was bordered with bottle-green Chinese junipers
that swayed gently together like green sailors on the lawn.

Fyodor Al-Din blinked his little eyes. His beak hung open.

Amidst the lawn, gorgeously mown in lines of sea-green
and olive-green, little fountains of yellow toi-tois
whispered and bobbled their frothy heads.
At each corner a corkscrew hazel tree flourished like a singer.

And in the middle a small pond fluted with lilies and light.

Fyodor Al-Din stared. Goose-stepping across the lawn,
its tail clattering and whirring in the sunshine,
was a peacock. It stopped. Fyodor held his breath.
Then it screamed at the neat hedges of shining honeysuckle.

Fyodor gulped. 'Bloody Hell,' he said.

For the next two days and nights he busied himself
building a nest in a hazel tree out of twigs, mud and grass
and lining it carefully with sweet wrappers, dogs' hairs,
silver paper from cigarette packets, moss and newspaper.

Then he fluffed down behind the leaves to watch the peacock.

The peacock did not notice Fyodor Al-Din.
Each morning it stamped up and down the garden
and then looked at itself for several hours in the pond,
squealing and shreiking at the trembling bullrushes and lilypads.

Fyodor shrank behind the twirly hazel branches.

At lunchtime the peacock would sleep with one eye open,
swivelling it slowly like the bore of a pistol.
Its beak glinted. Refreshed, the peacock would then
spend the afternoon posing amongst the spice-scented roses.

Then it pecked at their stems until they rocked and bled.

In the evening Mr and Mrs Golodin came home
and threw the peacock some expensive seeds and white grapes,
which it ignored; and then it marched about the hedges
barking and rattling its dazzling fan as the sun went down.

Mr and Mrs Golodin smiled, and went inside.

The peacock then gobbled up the grapes and the seeds,
snorted at the moon and stabbed its reflection in the pond.
Night wrapped the garden up in its dusky coat
and Fyodor Al-Din went to sleep in his new nest.

The peacock's eye glittered through the night.

One day, when the peacock was preening its electric-blue breast
Fyodor Al-Din bibbled down behind it, and combed his own.
When the peacock goose-stepped away to inspect the roses
Fyodor strutted, in a hopping way, behind it.

His little legs soon got tired, and he hid behind the bullrushes.

At sunset, when the peacock opened and elevated its tail
like a philharmonic organ, Fyodor did the same, and,
with the effort, broke wind. The peacock turned like a galleon
and glared at Fyodor Al-Din. 'Piss off!' it screamed.

Fyodor jumped backwards into the honeysuckle hedge.

For the next few days, he followed the peacock about,
rustling and strutting at a safe distance,
and soon he could hold up his little black head
and stamp up and down the lawn, following the sea-green lines.

And at night he slept with one eye open, until it closed.

One day, as he marched past the pond close behind the peacock,
Fyodor Al-Din stopped to look at his reflection
in the shiny water. He fluffled his black wings
and stuck out his little chest. The toi-tois whispered.

He turned. The peacock was right beside him.

Its eyes drilled into his own, zizzing with scorn.
Its tail looked like a poisonous rainbow.
'Get out!' hissed the peacock, flexing its claws,
'before I bite your head off.' Fyodor's little legs trembled.

'Excuse me,' he said, and goose-stepped across the lawn.

The peacock's scream of laughter was so loud
Mr and Mrs Golodin came running outside.
The sun dropped yellowly behind the honeysuckle hedge.
Fyodor Al-Din crashed through the bullrushes back to his nest.

His little heart banged faster than rain. The night hid him.

From then on he watched the peacock from the Chinese junipers
and at night he practised in the safety of a hazel tree.
Sometimes the peacock spat at him and did a vicious ballet-dance
on the grass around the bottom of the tree.

The scented seeds glittered on the grass.

When the cold weather came and the stars twinkled
through the smoke of Cherkesovo like needles,
Mr and Mrs Golodin caught the peacock in a large net
and carried it into the conservatory and shut the sliding doors.

Fyodor Al-Din flew down quietly onto the cold grass.

He watched it screaming at the potted palms,
its tongue flicking silently behind the glass.
The palm fronds quivered and shrank. The days shortened.
Dark-blue blinds were drawn all along the conservatory.

The first flakes of snow fell, pattering against the glass.

Fyodor Al-Din strutted in the corkscrew hazel tree
and screamed at the birds that flew high over the garden
in big Vs, but they took no notice. As the weather
grew colder he sank deeper and deeper into his nest.

He pushed his little head into the paper, which crackled with ice.

The dark-blue curtains stayed shut. Mr and Mrs Golodin
No longer came out into the snow-covered garden.
The pond froze over and bit off the remains of the bullrushes.
The flowers shrank and the trees ditched their leaves.

Fyodor Al-Din's little black eyes went glazed and waxy.

Sometimes at night, through the bare branches,
he could just make out the shadow of the peacock
trembling viciously, like a great fan,
three times life-size, against the curtain.

Clouds rolled over the rooftops, and he sighed.

Winter was so cold he nearly froze to death.
The garden sank into a big plate of ice.
A rook landed in the corkscrew hazel tree
and looked at Fyodor with his head on one side.

His little body was huddled up in a shivering heap.

'Come on,' said the rook, poking Fyodor gently with his foot.
'You're late.' Smoke swirled out of the chimneys all around.
Fyodor Al-Din stared at the crow and raised his head
haughtily out of the nest. 'Piss off,' he said.

The rook flew away into the sky with a million others.

He lived on rotten berries and frozen bits of bread
and rubbish dropped in the streets of Cherkesovo.
He pecked at dustbin bags and begged outside the cake-shop.
His feathers went oily and fragile; his eyes hard and ruthless.

And in the end, Spring lifted the snow away on its shoots.

One morning the dark-blue curtains opened.
Fyodor Al-Din flew down and pressed his beak against the glass.
Some peacock feathers stood twinkling in a green vase on the table;
a photo of the peacock, smiling poisonously, hung above the stove.

He watched and waited. But the peacock never appeared again.

Fyodor Al-Din kicked a hole in his nest and flew into town.
He marched up and down in front of the cake-shop and shreiked.
He waved his little tail until the feathers bent.
The shop-assistant threw some breadcrumbs at him across the
      pavement.

Fyodor stamped towards them and inspected them with a hard eye.

'That bird's a wierdo,' said the shop-assistant to his girlfriend
as they shared a cigarette in the sun. 'Do birds go mental?'
'I dunno,' said his girlfriend. 'It's only a bloody crow –
what's it got to go mental about then?' 'That's never a crow.'

The shop assistant stared. 'Don't be thick,' said his girlfriend.

Fyodor Al-Din never left Cherkesovo. The shop-assistant
and his girlfriend fed him every day and he goose-stepped
up and down amongst the bread trays and old newspapers,
holding up his head and squealing. One day he didn't come back.

'He's dead, innit?' said the girl.

The sky above Cherkesovo was black with smoke
which drifted away and got lost in the infinite air.
Mr Golodin mowed the lawn in neat sea-green and olive-green lines
and the first blue-black, speckled crows' eggs lay in their nests

up the larches in the fields on the banks of the Ulu-Yul.

*